Kyusho
Attack Points in Self defense an(

Acknowledgements

As authors of a joint project we're indebted to the following persons:

- Harald Marek M.A. (4th Dan Jujitsu) for his comprehensive work as photographer.
- Senior Consultant, Dr. Mehdi Mousavi (5th Dan Jujitsu) for the foreword and for taking a critical look at our work in the book.
- Dr. Thomas Hausner (6th Dan Karate-Do), Specialist for Trauma Surgery and Surgical Specialist at the UKH (Accident Hospital) Lorenz Böhler Vienna, for his input regarding the solar plexus and celiac plexus.
- Dr. Moritz Hawliczek (1st Dan Jujitsu) for his medical advice.
- Peter Rütter (5th Dan Shotokan Karate), Management Coach, lawyer, two- times World Vice-Champion in Karate for his assistance with the cover picture.
- Sebastian Rudigier (1st Dan Jujitsu) for acting as our model for the additional photos in the second edition.
- Alexandra Runge for the cover photo.
- Benjamin Schmid for being the "victim" for the additional photos in this edition.

Thanks to each of you!

Stefan + Juergen + Axel

Warning

This book contains some techniques that can be dangerous and must only be practiced under the supervision of a qualified trainer or instructor. The author and the publishers cannot be held responsible for any injuries that might result.

This book has been written using exclusively the male form of the personal pronoun. Of course, for reasons of simplicity this should be understood to include the female form as well.

Stefan Reinisch, Juergen Hoeller & Axel Maluschka

Kyusho

Attack Points in Self defense and Martial Arts

Meyer & Meyer Sport

Original title: Kyusho – Angriffspunkte in Selbstverteidigung und Kampfsport
Aachen: Meyer & Meyer, 3ʳᵈ edition, 2012

British Library Cataloguing in Publication Data
A catalogue record for this book is available from the British Library

Kyusho
Attack Points in Self defense and Martial Arts
Stefan Reinisch, Juergen Hoeller & Axel Maluschka
Maidenhead: Meyer & Meyer Sport (UK) Ltd., 2012
ISBN: 978-1-84126-361-8

© 2012 by Meyer & Meyer Sport (UK) Ltd.
Auckland, Beirut, Budapest, Cairo, Cape Town, Dubai, Indianapolis,
Kindberg, Maidenhead, Sydney, Olten, Singapore, Tehran, Toronto
Member of the World
Sport Publishers' Association (WSPA)
www.w-s-p-a.org
Printed by: B.O.S.S Druck und Medien GmbH
ISBN: 978-1-84126-361-8
E-Mail: info@m-m-sports.com
www.m-m-sports.com

Contents

Foreword Dr. Mehdi Mousavi

The martial arts from the Far East have enjoyed increasing popularity in the last few years. This fact is reflected in the numerous books, magazines, and other literature about Bushido that are flooding the market at the moment. However, forgetting the technical information, if you search for any works on the physical principles, anatomical physiological descriptions or even medical sports recommendations, you will be quickly disappointed. It is exactly these points, the so-called vital points, that cannot be learned without necessary knowledge of the anatomical facts and physiological regulatory mechanisms of the body. Many of these points are used as acupuncture points to cure various diseases, but several of these points can be life-threatening for the opponent. Only knowledge of these facts by the user can generate the necessary responsibility to be able to judge the situation correctly and react adequately to a possible attack.

The authors have attempted to illustrate and explain the anatomical basics of the vital points in this book through text and pictures. The way to use these points in self-defense by applying pressure on sensitive areas and their resulting effects are explained in detail. The dangers of using these vital points are based on medical factors.

The authors have succeeded for the first time in producing a medical/scientific-based work that matches the requirements of the reader from more than a technical aspect. Moreover, the book serves as a reference work for those exercising, covering how and where such pressure points can achieve best effects. Therefore, this book should be in every Budoka's library.

With long standing practice in the martial arts, I recommend the reader not underestimate the pressure points and stay in constant practice with them because only the correct precision in executing Kyusho can guarantee absolute and perfect defense. "He, who thinks he is good, stops trying to be better."

Dr. Mehdi Mousavi
Head of the Accident Surgical and Sports Accident Department of the Social Medical Center East-Donau Hospital in Vienna.
(5th Dan Jujitsu; Kawaishi Ryu)

Foreword Dr. Franz Knafl

As General Secretary of the European Jujitsu Union (E.J.J.U.) and President of Shobukai Austria, it is a pleasure for me to write the foreword to the third edition of Kyusho, which covers the sensitive points of the human body. It gives the interested reader a didactic, well-structured understanding and overview about the important pressure and vital points on the body and explains their efficiency and possible effects.

This specialized book shows many potential self-defense sequences and gives every person exercising new impulses for daily training. Simultaneously, it dispels many myths and is equally a call to cast a critical eye on this theme.

Even though the index of contents and explanations of the individual techniques cover attack points on the head, neck, torso, arms and legs, the aim is clear that the uses of Kyusho against an attacker are primarily for their use in defense.

The authors and their advisers have had much experience with the various Budo disciplines for many years. As practicing sportsmen of various far-eastern martial arts, they know well the theoretical and practical background for the precise and purposeful (according to the situation) application of Kyusho from their own practice and experience of the effects.

This textbook ideally serves to broaden the knowledge of both master and pupil. However, it cannot replace the necessary and responsible training with expert instructors and trained partners. Correct Jujitsu, Karate, Taekwondo and other martial arts demand unending and lifelong training.

Dr. Franz Knafl
8th Dan Jujitsu Kawaishi Ryu
General Secretary European Jujitsu Union
President Shobukai Austria Nippon Jujitsu Course
Head at the University Sports Institute Vienna (Universitäts-Sportinstitut Wien)

Introduction

"Five point palm-exploding heart technique" from Quentin Tarantino's film Kill Bill, Volume 2 (2004), Enter the Dragon (1973) with Bruce Lee, etc.

Whenever the subject of Asian martial arts comes up, sooner or later secretive techniques are alluded to that have been handed down only to the best students of the top masters. The legend of the "Touch of Death" could only have been created on the basis of a lack of knowledge by the average person regarding the anatomy of the human body – something that has clearly not changed much over time.

Although our knowledge about the composition of the human body has increased, in many books on the subject of martial arts, an explanation concerning the effect of various striking and pressure techniques has reduced to mentioning merely "causes pain, paralysis, death." Explanations are missing. Simply from a standpoint of personal responsibility for one's training partners (and from a legal point of view) it would be very welcome if the followers of martial arts delved more into the possible medical outcome of their actions.

The time delay of the effect of certain actions is of course part of the reason for the secretive aura of this aspect of martial arts. On the one hand, however, as every accident surgeon knows, the phenomena that symptoms arise comes a certain amount of time after the actual incident (e.g., internal injuries following a kick). On the other hand, a technique that has a delayed effect in an actual defense situation is not going to help one much. Nevertheless, such myths as these will never die simply because of the intriguing effect they have.

All defensive actions (irrespective of the individual martial art) are aimed at sensitive areas on the body (in Japanese, this is called "kyusho" – in Chinese martial arts, it is called "dim-mak") in order to make the opponent inactive as soon as possible. In the short term, the actions are mainly aimed at getting the attacker into a position where he will be vulnerable to follow-up techniques. While lever techniques are applied to the joints and can be used with appropriate, relative severity (pain or injury), the employment of the various striking, kicking pressure techniques is often not so easily controlled. The effects depend upon:

- The constitution of the opponent (it can be that delicate girls are not sensitive to the pain produced by nerve pressure techniques, while strong men collapse onto the floor as if lightning has struck them)
- Any previous injuries present
- Type of clothing being worn (e.g., a thick winter jacket)
- The precision of executing the technique
- The angle of attack
- The strength of the strike/kick/pressure
- Whether the action surprised the opponent. For example, attacks on surrounding nerves in the tense muscles are thus naturally difficult.

There are many vulnerable points on the human body. Some are called nerve points, others have an effect on the organs that are not protected by muscle tissue or bones, while in other cases there are mechanical weak points. Some of the points open the way for a follow-up action, while others end with the attack.

The effects are spread broadly and range from superficial pain or injury to death. The effects on the various points are totally different (also influenced by their accessibility) and this is why some of the listed target areas are interesting from a viewpoint of the Budo term "totality"– in a competition/fight they are of secondary importance. If, in spite of this, you have any doubts about the relevance of Kyusho in martial arts sports, you should consider that a boxer strives to hit his opponent at his vulnerable spots (chin, liver, and solar plexus). Punches to the kidneys, nape of the neck, or the genitals are, on the other hand, forbidden because they are considered as too dangerous in the framework of a sporting competition.

As a general maxim, previous effective techniques (e.g., the lever) can be complemented by using Kyusho which increases their effectiveness further. However, the enthusiasm must not be extended, in any case, so that the reliability of a technique suffers (along the lines of "For a hammer, every problem looks like a nail"). The most dangerous opponents are those who can turn the pain into aggressiveness or strength. Kyusho only makes sense when used in conjunction with other martial arts techniques.

TIP: If finding the point is somewhat difficult, it can be advantageous to look for it on your own body and feel its structure. Finding the point on a training partner's body is a little easier. Besides this, one learns very quickly to distinguish between the individual feelings of pain (for example, which nerves or muscles). To mark the target areas, the so-called "target plasters" have proved to be helpful in training.

The Results of Using Kyusho

Pain
In most cases, the opponent should be made to stop a particular action by applying pain (e.g., loosening his grip). Following this action is the opportunity to create "holes" for follow-up techniques. Sometimes pain is a side effect (e.g., the dislocation of a joint).

The International Association for the Study of Pain[1] defines pain as follows:

"Pain is an unpleasant sensory and emotional experience associated with actual or potential tissue damage, or described in terms of such damage."

Sensory perception is transmitted by **pain receptors** (nociceptors) down special nerve pathways and the thalamus to the central nerve system and this leads to the feeling of pain.

The distribution of these receptors across the surface of the body varies according to the body region (up to 200/sq cm of skin). Furthermore, one also finds nociceptors in the muscles and the lining of the intestines; the intestines themselves, as with the brain, have no pain receptors.

Some of the Kyusho techniques have an effect on the nerves and these can lead to uncontrollable signals (such as tingling on the side of the hand with the pinky finger when the nervus ulinaris is stimulated). In addition, it can lead to a tissue lesion of the nerve, as well as the nerve sheath, caused by the mechanical effect on the nerve. Besides this experience, pressure applied to these nerves can cause local and limited circulatory disorders and with it metabolic disorders that lead to extreme pain. Rapid relief is typical once the mechanical problem is removed. One possible complication is the inflammation of the nerve (neuritis).

Pain caused by an effect is called **neuralgia** and spreads through the area supplied for each nerve (innervation area).

The more often a respective nerve is stimulated, the more sensitively it reacts to stimulation and the feeling of targeted pain is increased as a result.

Not every physical injury leads ultimately to pain. This is because of the filter processes in our central nervous system (stress reliefs or injuries resulting from a traffic accident, competition, war or during sexual intercourse are often not noticed)[2] , while on the other hand pain without physical injury can also occur (e.g., phantom pain).

Pain resulting in unconsciousness

Pain can result not only from a physical injury, but it can also lead to unconsciousness. This is called a vasovagal syncope (other causes can be anxiety, joy or other types of excitement; also called the "Boygroup-syndrome").

The cause is an overreaction in the vegetative nervous system. An enlargement of the blood vessels, so that (above all) the blood "seeps away" into the intestines and a relative lack of volume with decreased heartbeat rate occurs, caused by the decrease in venous flow back of blood to the heart. On the other hand it leads to a reduction of the heart rate up to even cardiac arrest. This results in an overall reduction of the supply of blood and/or oxygen to the brain with subsequent fainting occurring.

A vasovagal syncope resulting in death is called reflexogenic cardiac arrest. Further reasons for a death of this kind of fatal circulatory collapse (especially concerning Martial Arts) can be: the Carotid Sinus syndrome following a blow on the carotid artery in the neck, the oculocardiac reflex following a blow in the eyes, a strike or kick at the solar plexus or a kick in the testicles. To make a distinction, however, unconsciousness due to a craniocerebral trauma is quite clearly different to a vasovagal syncope!

The effects of acupuncture

Let us look at the possible effects in connection with acupuncture and their meridian points. It is in this area, however, where much controversy exists between experts in the martial arts. We will therefore try to briefly illustrate the different perspectives.

On the one hand, there is an opinion that the effects are **psychological** and **physiological** ones:

An example of this is where, in Germany, the health insurance company accepts the costs of acupuncture treatment for patients with knee and back pains. The decision made by the national health insurance company is based on studies carried out by the Charité-Universitätsmedizin Berlin on a model framework of 250,000 test subjects and 10,000 physicians (up to now the largest study on the subject of acupuncture in Germany. According to the results of the study, the rate of success for traditional Chinese acupuncture (or TCM, traditional Chinese medicine, – "genuine" acupuncture) in the treatment of chronic back pain is not much more than that achieved using "sham" acupuncture (placebo acupuncture), where "false" points are "treated." However, both forms of acupuncture showed distinctly better success than the standard therapy.

In short, acupuncture actually does work. Where you put the needle in seems not to play a significant role.

Therefore, we come to the question on what its effectiveness is based. This is where the **placebo effect**[3] comes into play. Dr. Michael Freissmuth, University Professor on the Board of the Pharmakologischen Instituts der Medizinischen Universität (Pharmacological Institute of the Medical University) Vienna, sees this as a clear indication of the physician's "bedside manner." This is also similar to statements made by Dr. Fabricio Benedetti, a Neurobiologist in Turin, where he sees the context in which the patient is treated as being crucial. The physician's manner can work on the chemistry of the brain, such that this has a positive effect on the whole organism.[4] The placebo effect is not just simply a psychological one ("illusion"). On the contrary, concrete biological changes in the body can be measured as a result of it.

Of course, many analogies can be suggested between the "Professor" in a physician's white coat and the "Grand Master" with the black belt. Many martial arts masters even reckon that they can create a K.O. at a "distance" without touching their opponent.[5] Perhaps one may have the image of an American television preacher who jumps around through the crowd of believers and lays his hand on the next person, who sinks down to the ground as if struck by the Holy Ghost (see the "Boygroup" syndrome on the previous page). Ritual, symbols, and authority all play a major part in this area. Otherwise, why would the doctor rush about with a stethoscope around his neck? This has the same effect as the shaman with his rattle or the red/white belt of the highly qualified martial arts master: "The man/woman is an authority – I can already feel the effect!"

Just how far this trust in perceived authority can go was illustrated impressively in the classic Milgram experiment in 1961 (sadly, it has been repeated several times with the original results since then).

The behavior of the other group or training members also, however, has a strong influence on one's own behavior ("social reinforcement").

On the other hand, there are the followers of the mode of working with "ki" (or "chi"), yin and yang energy fields. However, these concepts from the Far East must also always be seen in their cultural background. Those inexperienced in the field of anatomy would describe the pain from knocking the "funny bone," or more precisely the "nervus ulnaris"(ulnar nerve), as a flow of energy. Yin and yang also have a parallel in neurology through the sympathetic and parasympathetic nerve system.[6] The reason that they specialize in the use of nerve points in martial arts, often attacking several points simultaneously or one after the other (for examples, see books by George Dillman and Michael Kelly), lies in the fact that the stimulation creates an added effect and thus increases its effectiveness.[7] The consequences arising from this are completely impressive because of the effect on the internal organs. (For the neurological background on this, we recommend reading Dr. Michael Kelly's book Death Touch: The Science Behind the Legend of Dim-Mak.

However, this is where the person training is at a disadvantage: How can you train realistically in a martial art where the main aim is to cause the opponent to become unconscious or suffer heart failure or a heart attack? The possibility of testing the effectiveness of these techniques on convicts – like the "Masters" of many years ago were reported to have done – is, thankfully now nonexistent. Also a "simple knock-out," as shown often in many courses on the subject of Kyusho/Dim-Mak, can have lethal consequences if there are pre-existing health defects.[8] If you wish to remain on the right side of legal and ethical rules, training of this kind has to remain as just theory.[9] The practical difficulties cannot also be underestimated: The effectiveness should be much more when more nerve points are stimulated. This can be up to a combination of five techniques (does this ring a bell?) that all have to be carried out in the correct sequence and precisely located. The possibilities and reasons are, of course, fascinating but the practical relevance is questionable.

The stretch reflex

Muscle spindles are sensory receptors (so-called "proprioreceptors") within the muscle that primarily detect changes in the length of this muscle. They also protect the muscle from overstretching. When the muscle is suddenly stretched, the so-called "stretch reflex" is activated and the muscle retracts again. The more sudden the stretching action occurs, the more muscle fibers are activated in the muscle spindles and the greater the power that counteracts against the stretching of the muscle. The so-called Golgi tendon organ, however, also contributes to this by transmitting the changes of tension in the tendons.

Example:
One nods off and the head falls forward. At the same time, the head whips back upward as a result of the sudden overstretch of the neck muscles. Another example is the knee-jerk triggered by the tiny physician's hammer.

Particularly in our case, our striking techniques are amplified by this type of reflex where they can be accompanied by circumstanced nerve pain.

Examples:

- A strike on the outside of the lower arm (for more detail see the section on this) acts on the nervus radialis, which is responsible for the movement of stretching the fingers. The stretching reflex activates those muscles that are also responsible for the movement of the fingers, which is why the hand opens or, at least, is weakened.
- A strike on the biceps (for more detail see the section on this) causes the arm to bend in accompaniment with the inertia.
- A strike at the insertion point of the sternokleido muscle (for more detail see the section on this) and the temporal bone rattles the head at least as hard as when one is hit on the bone (mastoid process).

For a better overview, it has proven best to divide the attack areas into five regions, namely those on the head, neck, torso, arms and the legs. The most easily reachable targets are on the head and about the neck – so this is why we have begun with these areas.

One note in advance: The evaluation of the applicability is usually done without taking into account legal or moral aspects.

1   Attack Points on the Head

1.1   Eyes

This concerns those targets that are protected by our instincts (like the testicles), where even a faked movement toward them (protective reflex by the hands) prompts a reaction from the attacker and often leaves the door open for follow-up actions. An illustration of this is hardly necessary.

Attack: The effect is created by pressure or a jab with the fingers, but also possible by punching.

2   Control of the elbow
The elbow is pressed in and downward toward the attacker's body.

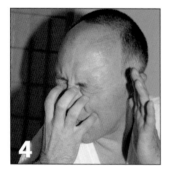

Effects: Severe contusions of the eyeball lead to serious injuries to the inner structure of the eye: internal bleeding of the eye caused by vascular lesions; increase of the eye pressure (possibly resulting in glaucoma problems); tears in the iris (pupil is no longer circular); blurring or displacement of the lens; tears in the retina with danger of retinal detachment; swelling of the retina with reduced vision and damage to the optic nerve.

The effect of a strike or pressure on the optic nerve (nervus opticus) can have a follow through effect on the nervous system that results in a reduction in heart frequency, unconsciousness, and/or cardiac arrest. This is also known as oculocardiac reflex or Aschner phenomenon.

When struck, it is also possible that fractures of the orbital bone structures surrounding the eyeball can occur with damage to the nerves and blood vessels (can also lead to reduced vision if the eyeball is displaced).

Gouging out the eyeball cavity (Latin: orbita) with the fingers is, however, almost as good as impossible.

Further effects can include uncontrollable flow of tears (although this can cause limited vision), pain, and eventual unconsciousness (as a result of the pain).

Indirect effects: with compression of the eyeball (Latin: bulbus), detachment of the retina can occur. The effect of this is that a person temporarily sees flickering white spots in their field of vision, which disappear after a time. In the vernacular, one speaks of "spots before their eyes" or seeing "stars" or spots "dancing" before their eyes.

Comments on use:
As far as effects being achieved with the minimum use of force and effectiveness, it concerns targets of the first order. The constitution of the other person is of no import. The move can be used as far as the arms can reach.

Variations:

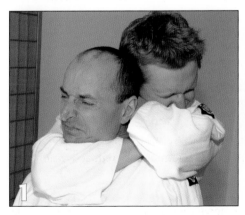 

1   Attack using an Ushiro jime (stranglehold in the crook of the forearm).
2   Defense using the thumbs to apply pressure on the eyes.

Variations:

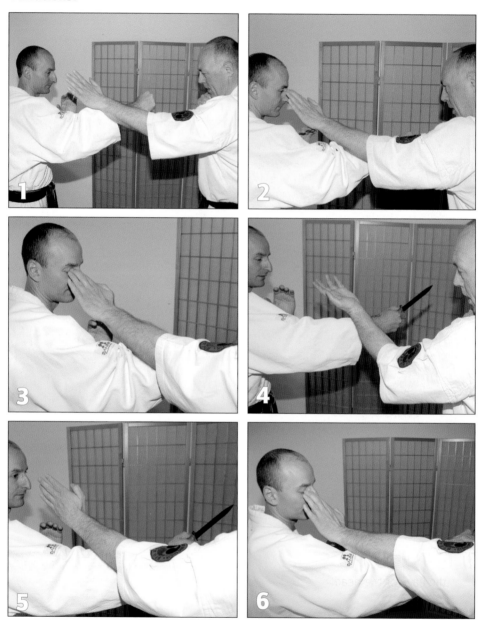

1   Making contact with the attacking arm.
2   The attacker's arm serves as a conducting rail for the defending arm as it rides up it to jab the attacker's eye with the spear of the finger.

1.2   Chin/Protuberancia mentalis

The protuberancia mentalis is the three-cornered protuberance of the chin bone.

Attack: Pressure with the joint of the thumb (the tip of the thumb should be anchored to the forefinger).

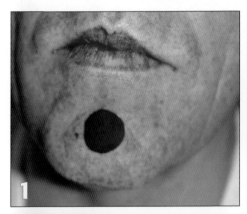

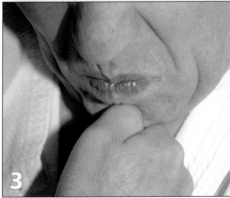

1   Target mark.
2   Usage. The tip of the thumb is pressed into the point of the chin. The hand holds the back of the head.
3   Close-up.

Effects: Pain (the periosteum, or skin membrane, is very sensitive to pain)

Comments on use:
Only use as a freeing technique – further techniques should follow.

1.3 Corners of the mouth

Attack: Crooking the finger in one or both sides of the corners of the mouth and pulling outward.

1   Freeing from the scarf hold (Kesa Gatame).

Effects: Pain, ripping of the lips.

Comments on use:
Frees the hold shown reliably; possible risk of endangering one's self (teeth!).

Variation:

 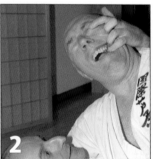 

1   Attacking the eye as well as the corners of the mouth.

1.4 Nose bone/Root of the nose/Os nasale

Illustration – see the section on the "Skull."

The nose bone is in the front of the skull, roughly about where a pair of eyeglasses sits. The nose bone is particularly thin and project out seemingly unprotected from the face of the skull.

Attack: Strike (using the fist, hammer fist, ball of the hand, side of the hand, temple). Pressure is applied using the fore and middle fingers in a scissor grip but focused more on the cartilaginous extremities area under the nose bone.

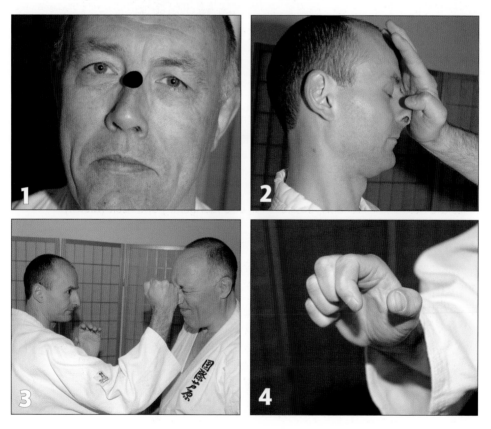

1 Target mark.   **2** Attack with the ball of the hand.   **3** Attack using a hammer fist.
4 The scissor grip using the knuckles.

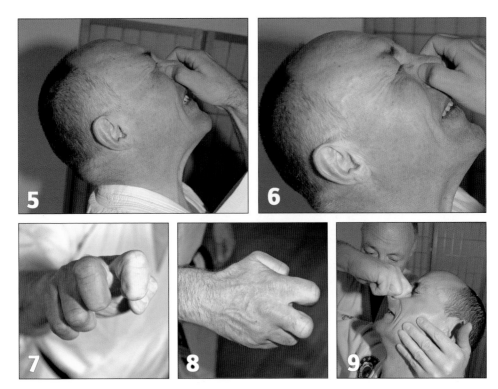

5 Usage.   **6** From another viewpoint.   **7/8** The scissor grip using the knuckles.
9 Usage.

Effects: Even light blows can cause a fracture of the nose bone and nasal cartilage. The results are extreme pain (the nervi ethmoidales posterior and anterior supply sensory information to the nasal mucous membrane and the tip of the nose), the eyes begin to water (limiting sight). If the nose bleeds, blood can flow into the pharynx and, in an extreme case, block the passage of air.

Furthermore, in a blow to the nose, the cartilaginous part of the nasal septum can slide out of its bony guide groove (subluxation). Legend says that a blow to the nose can "push" the nose bone into the brain.

Injury to the sinuses is also possible with subsequent infection. See also section on "Skull."

Comments on use:

Typical injuries suffered from a "brawl" that do not necessarily stop the attack depending on the ability to take blows. In an attack where pressure is used, a counter with the other hand is necessary (nape of the neck, chest, and lumbar part of the spine).

Examples:

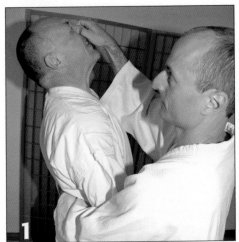

1   Scissor grip on the nose combined with the back being bent over to the rear.
2   Defense against a fist attack.
3   Defensive arm moves up to take a scissor grip on the attacker's nose.
4   Scissor grip while controlling the neck.

9 Using a kick to the inside of the opponent's knee joint, the attacking arm is stretched and thus allows an arm lever to be applied.

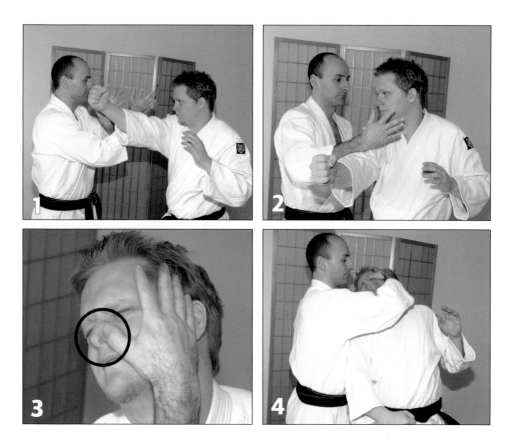

1   Defend against the fist attack.
2   Pressure with the thumb on one side of the edge of the nose bone.
3   Close-up.
4   Control and throw.

1.5   Subnasal point

Illustration – see the section on the "Skull."

The anatomical term for the vertical channel between the upper lip and the nose is *philtrum*. At its upper extremity, it extends to meet the bridge of the nose (columella – Latin: 'small column') to form the nasolabial angle. The pain comes from the local pain receptors.

Attack: Strike or pressure with the edge of the hand/thumb.

3   Beginning of the stretch-over phase.
5   Counter hold and thrust on the thigh. Pin down the body in order to prevent escape.

8   Controlling position stretching out the attacker.

Effect: Using a strike, the more harmless results are a cut lip and teeth knocked out. It is also possible to break the upper jaw bone (maxilla) as well as dislodge the cartilaginous nasal septum out of its bony groove. With hefty strikes, the usual injury effects to the skull (see the next section on the 'Skull') are possible, as with any hit on the head. Blood and broken teeth can enter the airways and hinder breathing.

When pressure is applied, nerve pain can be felt (neuralgia) (see the statements in the Introduction).

Comments on use:
There is a danger of injuring one's self (teeth). In an attack using pressure, a counter-hold with the other hand is necessary (on the neck, chest or lumbar spine).

Additional Sequences:

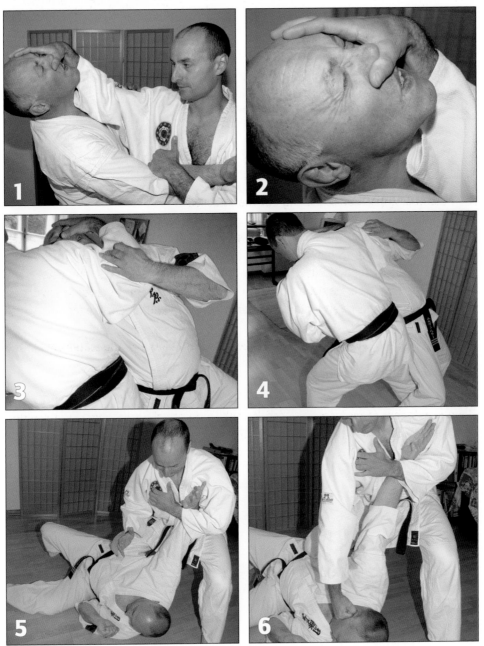

1 Stretching out while at the same time pinning the defender's arm against the body.
3 Continuation of the major outer reaping throw (O-soto-gari).
6 Conclusion.

1.6 Great auricular nerve/Nervus auricularis magnus

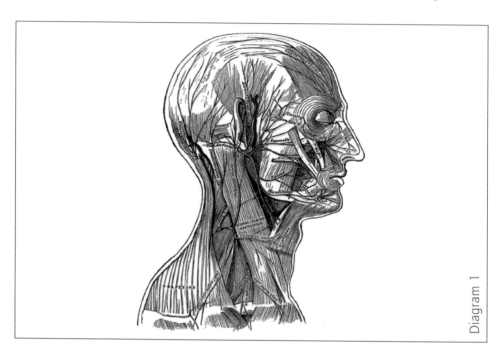

Diagram 1

Location: Behind the earlobes, at the rear of the jaw bone.

Attack: Pressure of the finger upward in the direction of the center of the skull (better control achieved when applied on one side with the palm of the other hand controlling the head.) Throw.

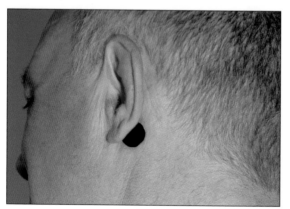

Tip: A rotating, boring, and rubbing pressure in the direction of the center of the head is better than constant pressure because the body adjusts less well to non-constant pain.

Target mark.

Effects: When pressure is applied, nerve pain can be felt (neuralgia) (see the statements in the Introduction).

Comments on use:
Like all nerve points, the degree of sensitivity and effectiveness is individually different.

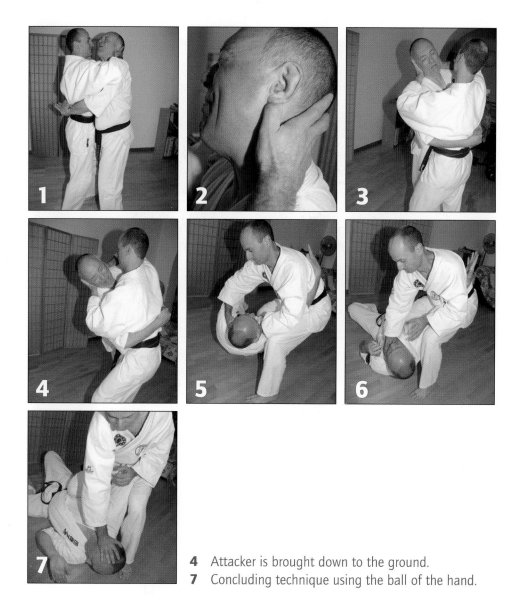

4 Attacker is brought down to the ground.
7 Concluding technique using the ball of the hand.

1.7   Buccal (cheek) nerve/Nervus buccalis

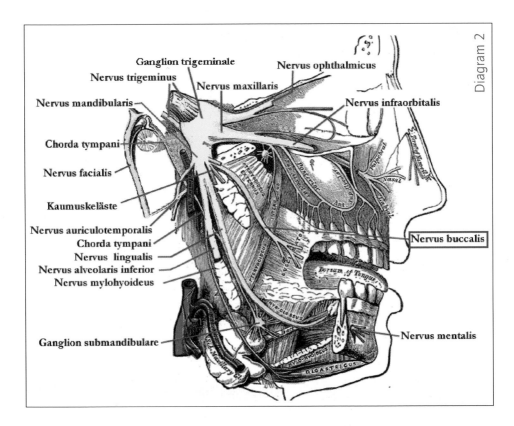

Diagram 2

Compare with the diagram in the section on the "Nervus frontalis."

The nervus buccalis (buccal/cheek nerve) is sensitive and supplies the mucous membranes of the cheeks as well as the gums.

Attack: Scissor grip below the cheekbone.

Effect: When pressure is applied, nerve pain can be felt (neuralgia) (see the statements in the Introduction).

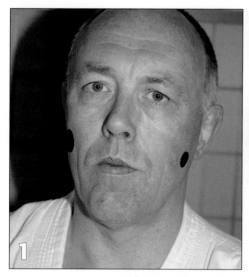 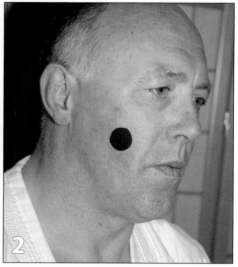

1 Target mark.

Comments on use:
Like all nerve points, the degree of sensitivity is individually different.

  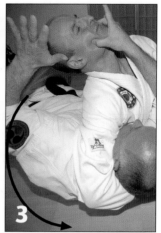

3 The attacker is stretched out from the pain.

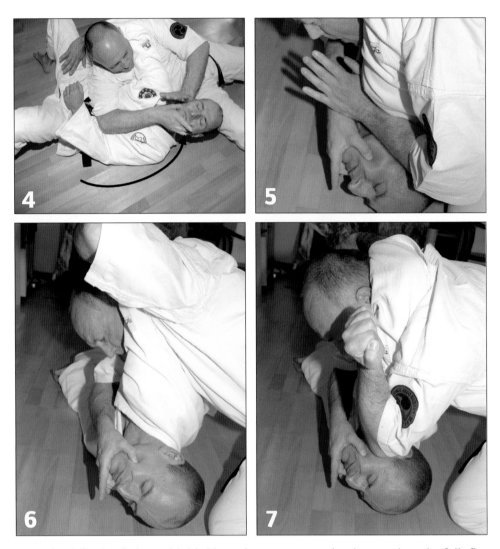

4 The defender dodges with his hip and turns away under the attacker who falls flat on the ground and can now be controlled.

5 Pinning him to the ground.

7 Concluding technique.

Possibilities of use when standing

1 The strike is diverted.

2 Using a scissor grip on the nervus buccalis and holding the back of the neck, the attacker is brought down to the ground with a blocking knee hook.

3 In the depicted defense position, an alternative to the scissor grip is one-sided pressure applied with the knuckle of the forefinger...

4 ...or the thumb.

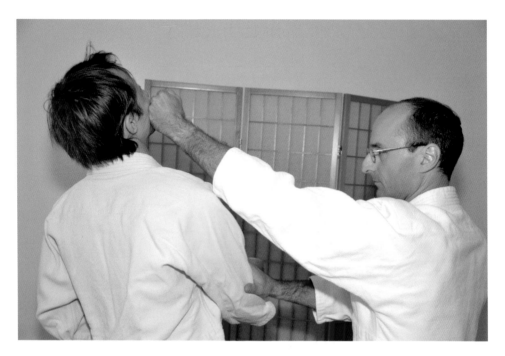

A punch can also be used with the knuckles of the little and ring finger striking the nervus buccalis. Besides pain caused to the nerve, there is also the pain to the skin of the cheek bone as well as the usual results of any strike to the head.

1.8 Forehead nerve/Nervus frontalis

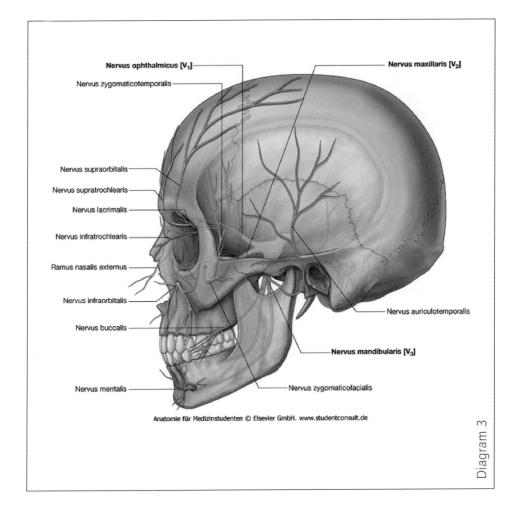

Nervus ophthalmicus [V$_1$]

Nervus maxillaris [V$_2$]

Nervus zygomaticotemporalis

Nervus supraorbitalis

Nervus supratrochlearis

Nervus lacrimalis

Nervus infratrochlearis

Ramus nasalis externus

Nervus infraorbitalis

Nervus buccalis

Nervus auriculotemporalis

Nervus mandibularis [V$_3$]

Nervus mentalis

Nervus zygomaticofacialis

Anatomie für Medizinstudenten © Elsevier GmbH. www.studentconsult.de

Diagram 3

The nervus frontalis (as well as the two terminal branches, nervus supraorbitalis and nervus supratrochlearis) runs along the outer eye muscles to the upper edge of the eye socket and emerges at the surface (at the start of the eyebrow or at the highest point of the eye socket – supraorbital foramen) where they are vulnerable.

Attack: Finger pressure (applied to the region of the eye socket) and strike (at the eyebrows).

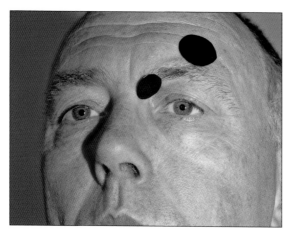

Target mark.

Effects: Nerve pain (neuralgia) can be felt after pressure applied (or after a punch) (see the statements in the Introduction).

Comments on use:
Take care with eye injuries. When pressure is applied, it is necessary to place the other hand at the back of the neck, on the chest or the lumbar spine, to counterbalance.

1   The attacker grabs the lapel of the jacket and threatens with his fist.
2   The defender punches over the attacking arm to hit the nerve on the temple with the knuckles (Hiraken).

3 Close-up. **4** The attacker's elbow is pinned at the same time. **5** Close-up.
6 The attacker's head is turned away from the defender. **7** The attacker is bent over...
8 ...and brought down to the ground.

10 Kick with the knee and pin the head to the ground.

Variations:

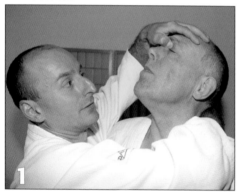 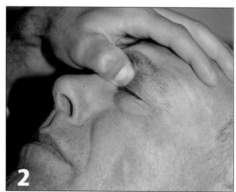

1 Defend using counter-balancing hand on the neck. The attacker's neck is pinned down.

 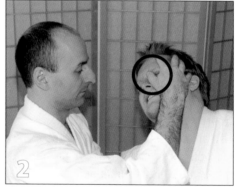

1 The swinging punch is deflected.

2 The striking arm is pinned, and the thumb applies pressure to the inside of the corner of the eye. Throw.

1.9   Infraorbital nerve/Nervus infraorbitalis

See "Nervus auricularis magnus," "Nervus frontalis," and "Nervus buccalis" illustrations. Direct continuation of the nervus maxillaris (maxillar branch) that is responsible for the sensitive innervation of the anterior skull. The nervus infraorbitalis emerges from the upper jaw about one finger-width below the eyes on the foramen infraorbitale. It can be felt in this area. After emerging from the hole, it branches out into the membranes of the skin on the whole front and upper face and transmits sensitivity to the upper lip, teeth, and gums of the upper jaw (see the section on the "Subnasal point").

Attack: Finger pressure/knuckle punch on the exit area.

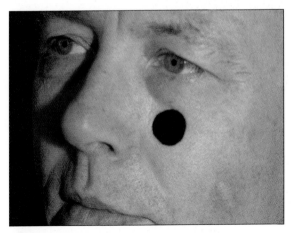

Target mark.

Effects: Nerve pain (neuralgia) can be felt after pressure is applied (see the statements in the Introduction).

Comments on use:
Like all nerve points, the degree of sensitivity, as well as the effect achieved, is individually different. When punching, a precise target is necessary (best executed using the knuckle of the forefinger).

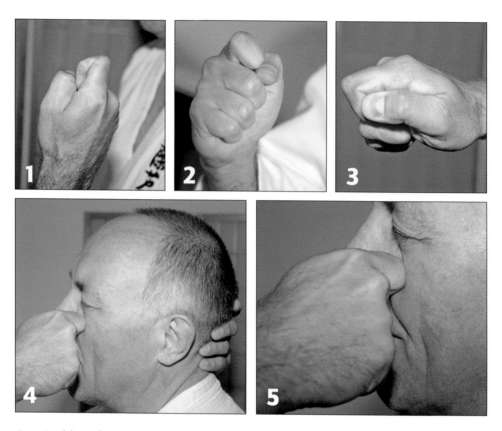

1   Position of the hand in Ipponken.
4   The effect of the attack is increased by pinning the back of the head with the free hand.
5   Close-up.

1.10   Mental nerve/Nervus mentalis

See the sections on the "Nervus frontalis" and "Nervus buccalis" for illustrations.

Terminal branch of the nervus alveolaris inferior. It emerges from the lower jaw bone at the chin (foramen mentale) and innervates the skin and membranes of the lower lip and chin.

Attack: Pressure using the knuckles (thumb), punch.

Punch:

1 The punch using the knuckles of the fingers is executed whip-like downward and serves as a shock tactic and as the beginning for further actions.

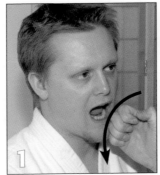

This technique opens the jaws whereby the joint is more vulnerable to injury from the follow-up punching techniques (see the section on the "Lower jaw").

Effects: Nerve pain (neuralgia) can be felt after pressure applied (see the statements in the Introduction).

Comments on use:
Like all nerve points, the degree of sensitivity, as well as the effect achieved is individually different. Usage is limited to this individual case.

Pressure using the knuckles:

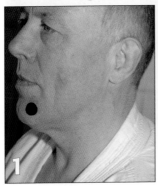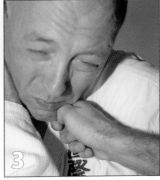

1 Target mark.

2 Way of holding the hand for follow-up attacks; the other hand is anchored at the back of the neck.

Further sequence:

1   The attacker's strike is defended using a double block.

2   The defender's right hand slides down the line of the arm being defended toward the attacker's chin.

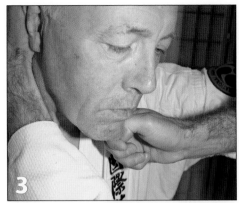

3   Strike.

6   Caused by pressure on the nerve, the attacker's head is turned and his body follows.

7   The attacker is brought down to the ground.

47

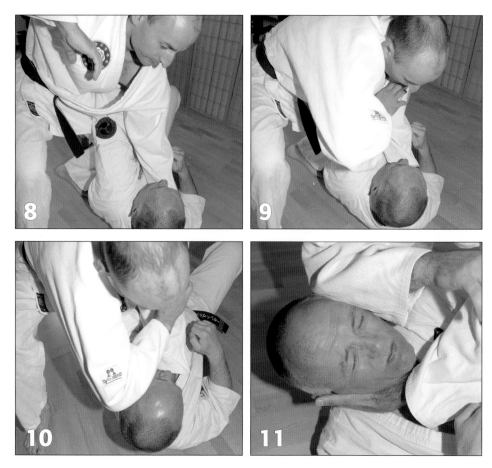

11 Concluding technique is a strike using the elbow.

1.11 Upper lip

Attack: Scissor grip on the upper lip.

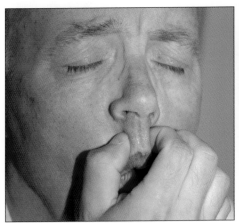 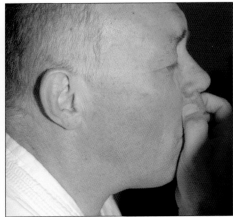

Effects: Pain caused by the effect on the musculus orbicularis oris (the circular segments of muscle around the mouth), namely the pain receptors and the infraorbital nerve (see the illustration in the sections on the "Nervus auricularis magnus" and "Nervus frontalis") that stretch through the upper jaw and innervate the teeth in the upper jaw, the gums and the upper lip. Nerve pain (neuralgia) can be felt after pressure is applied (see the statements in the Introduction).

Comments on use:
It is necessary that the other hand is used as a counter thrust (neck, chest/lumbar spine).

1.12   Ear

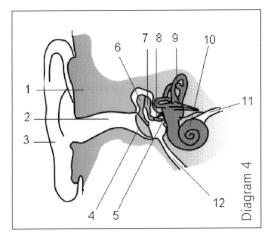

(1) Petrous bone (2) External auditory cavity (3) Ear flaps (4) Tympanic membrane – this is a thin membrane at the inner end of the auditory cavity, which closes it off from the middle ear (6) Malleus bone (7) Incus (8) Stape bone (stirrup) (9) Labyrinth (semicircular canals) – this is part of the inner ear and serves as the organic system for balance (10) Cochlea (11) Cochlea nerve (12) Eustachian tube

Diagram 4

Attack: Slap with a cupped hand at the ear (possibly with both hands) (practice using it against the partner's upper arms). Stick a finger in the auditory canal.

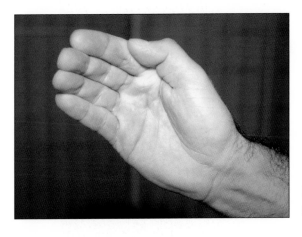

Form the cupped hand for the slapping action.

Effects: The eardrum vibrates due to sound waves – more precisely through the change of pressure caused by the sound – and this is transmitted from the ear ossicle in the middle ear to the inner ear. The slap with the cupped hand causes compression of the air in the auditory canal so that overpressure (barotrauma) occurs.

Apart from the noise, in addition to the rapid, strong and painful pressure, the eardrum can be ruptured. A ruptured eardrum usually heals itself, however this may also need to be repaired by an operation.

The effect described, however, is accompanied by pain: Several nerve branches are involved in the innervation of the eardrum, in particular the ramus auricularis, the vagus nerve and the nervus auriculotemparalis, a branch of the nervus trigeminus. The interior of the eardrum is innervated by the branches of the network of nerves in the membranes (plexus tympanicus) of the middle ear. Merely touching the eardrum is painful and, in some cases, can cause a feeling of nausea and even unconsciousness. An acute, sharp pain is typical in a traumatic perforation of the eardrum. A sudden reduction in hearing can also occur (depending on the degree of perforation). Germs can enter the middle ear through the perforation (mainly from water) and slight bleeding can also occur.

Because the inner ear is also involved in such a strike, this can also influence one's sense of balance and additionally be the cause of dizziness (vestibular dizziness).The dizziness is often accompanied by a vegetative reaction in the body, such as nausea, vomiting, sweating, cardio acceleration, and/or collapse.

Apart from the medical effects, sticking a finger in the ear causes a large reflex action (innervated by several brain nerves).

Comments on use:
Not much strength is required to create a significant effect.

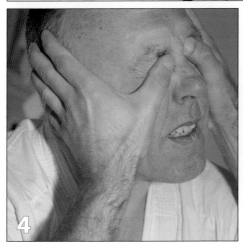

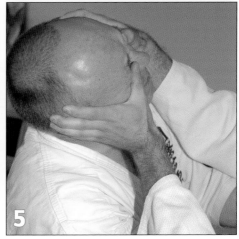

4 Directly after slapping the ear, the thumbs are thrust into the eyes.

5 The head is turned to the side with constant pressure on the eyeball.

9 Concluding technique: Strike with the elbow.

1.13   Parotid gland/Parotis

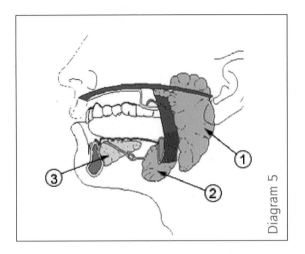

Diagram 5

1. *Glandula parotidea*
2. *Glandula submandibularis*
3. *Glandula sublingualis*

The parotid is the largest salivary gland in the oral and jaw region. In humans, it lies on both sides of the face in front of and below the ear, stretching down from the zygomatic arch to the angle of the jaw and covers the rear half of the masticatory muscle (musculus masseter). In the parotid is the so-called plexus parotideus, which is made of fibers from the nervus facialis. The sensitive innervation of the parotid comes from the nervus auriculotemporalis (see the illustration in the section on the "Nervus frontalis").

Attack: Pressure from the fingers, punch with the knuckles.

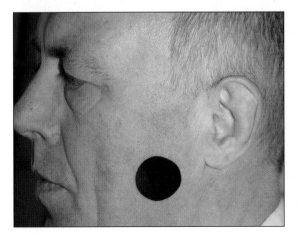

Target mark.

This is how to hold the hand for the knuckle punch. Strike with the upper side of the knuckles of the fist (Kento – 'sword fist'). The effect is increased by doing a snap movement outward from the wrist.

Effects: Muscle and nerve pain (neuralgia) can be felt after pressure is applied (see the statements in the Introduction). Besides this, the glandular tissue can be damaged. In a punch, damage to the lower jaw is also possible (for results see section on this).

Comments on use:
Like all nerve points, the degree of sensitivity and effectiveness is individually different.

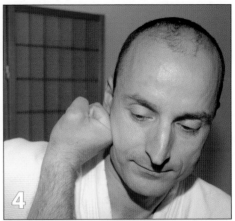

8 At the end of the sequence, the opponent is thrust to the ground.

An **additional combination** where the knuckles of the fingers are used to strike (Ryuto Ken Tsuki).

1   Defense.
2   Circular counter-movement with the fingers of the knuckle.
3   Using a whip-like strike, the parotid is possibly damaged, or at least the strike causes pain.

In this sequence, the knuckle of the thumb is used to strike.

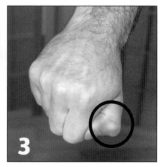

1.14   Skull

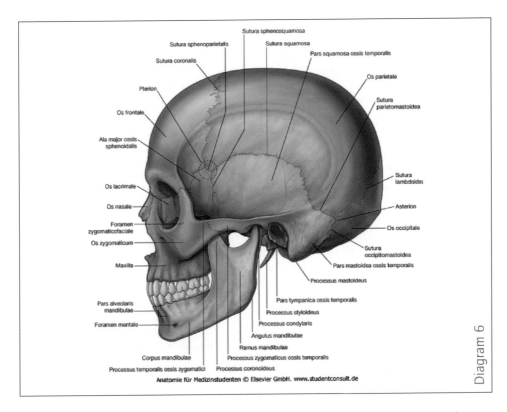

Sutura sphenosquamosa
Sutura sphenoparietalis
Sutura squamosa
Sutura coronalis
Pars squamosa ossis temporalis
Pterion
Os parietale
Os frontale
Sutura parietomastoidea
Ala major ossis sphenoidalis
Os lacrimale
Sutura lambdoidea
Os nasale
Asterion
Foramen zygomaticofaciale
Os occipitale
Os zygomaticum
Sutura occipitomastoidea
Maxilla
Pars mastoidea ossis temporalis
Processus mastoideus
Pars tympanica ossis temporalis
Pars alveolaris mandibulae
Processus styloideus
Foramen mentale
Processus condylaris
Angulus mandibulae
Ramus mandibulae
Corpus mandibulae
Processus zygomaticus ossis temporalis
Processus temporalis ossis zygomatici
Processus coronoideus

Anatomie für Medizinstudenten © Elsevier GmbH. www.studentconsult.de

Diagram 6

Attack: Strikes (careful not to damage one's own hands), kicks (using the knee).

1   Warding off the opponent's attack.
2   Controlling the elbow and the neck.
3   The attacker is brought down onto the knee.
5   The defender continues controlling the head and using his body to block the attacker's left arm.
6   Strike with the elbow at the back of the head.

Effects: Fractured skull and traumatic brain injury.

Types of skull fracture:
Basal skull fracture: At its base, the skull is connected to the neck spine. A fracture in this region often has the result of causing damage to the nerves of the brain where these emerge from the skull at the basal area. Sometimes cerebrospinal fluid flows

from the ear or nose and is often accompanied by disorientation or unconsciousness. A typical symptom is two black eyes (bilateral orbital hematoma).

Fracture of the bones of the facial skull: This includes the region of the eye sockets, the nasal bone and the upper and lower jaw. A fracture in these areas often causes the disruption of small bones in the area of the face and considerable swelling.

A **fracture of the eye socket** can lead to disrupted vision if the eyeball is displaced. Fractures of the skull cap (cranium) are possible, for example, after a major impact with the ground.

Where there is displacement of the broken bones, or splintering of bones in the interior skull cap occurs, these can penetrate deeply into the brain.

Craniocerebral injury (traumatic brain injury, or TBI) refers to all injuries to the cranium where the brain is also involved in the injury, but not to those injuries where there are no genuine skull fractures or head wounds. Because of the danger of internal bleeding in the brain, any patient suffering a traumatic brain injury (even concussion) must be taken to hospital for observation.

There are several methods used to classify the severity of traumatic brain injury (TBI). For the purpose of this book we, the authors, have chosen to list the grades and describe them along the lines of the system used in Germany. The descriptions below do not vary much between many of the systems and should be sufficient to give the reader an overview:

Injuries are described in three grades of severity, dependent upon the length of unconsciousness, remission of symptoms and any later complications:

- Grade 1: TBI (Commotio cerebri – brain concussion): This is defined as a light brain injury (i.e., with the cerebral membrane of the brain still intact) without loss of consciousness or unconsciousness up to an hour. Condition is completely healed after approximately five days. Generally, patients complain about moments of retrograde amnesia (lapses of memory) and nausea.

- Grade 2: TBI (Contusio cerebri – cerebral contusion): Loss of consciousness up to 24 hours. Complications depend on the area of brain damage.

- Grade 3: TBI (Compressio cerebri – cerebral compression): Unconsciousness longer than 24 hours caused by compression on the brain resulting in bleeding (increase in pressure, cerebral swelling). There can be intervals of minutes to hours where symptoms are absent. The results are often a long period of coma (sometimes artificially induced), a condition similar to a coma, respiratory paralysis or even death. In such cases, therapy involves the temporary removal of a part of the cranium (several months).

  Long-lasting damage can be expected, but this is not inevitable.

The following symptoms point to a traumatic brain injury. It should be noted that some of the symptoms listed can develop well after the actual trauma.

- Disturbance of consciousness, with possible deterioration
- Headaches
- Dizziness and loss of balance
- Cross-eyed state
- Difference in pupil size (differences between sizes of both pupils)
- Nausea and vomiting
- Unconsciousness
- Lapses of memory, amnesia
- Paralysis
- Irregularity of breathing and pulse
- Shock
- Motor and sensory disorders (e.g., tingling sensation)

Here the differences in pupil size and the increase of cases of disturbance in consciousness must be taken as warning signs because these may be an indication of internal bleeding in the cranium. However, unconsciousness is not always a sign of a traumatic injury to the frontal lobes. Nevertheless, such injuries can lead to long-lasting damage (e.g., frontal lobe disorders, cognitive disorders, behavioral disorders).

Comments on use:
Quite considerable skill or strength is necessary to execute these moves. Nevertheless, the area of the head is instinctively a preferred target for unskilled fighters.

1.15   Temporal bone

The temporal bone forms the osseous part of the temples (see the illustration in the section on the "Skull"). The temples (Latin: regio temporalis) are regions on the side of the head between the eye and the ear. These areas are very sensitive to blows because the middle ear, inner ear, and brain lie beneath the bone. These areas are also sensitive to pressure due to the presence of the nervus auriculotemporalis, the nervus zygomaticus, as well as the musculus temporalis (see the illustration in the section on the "Nervus frontalis").

In addition to the results described in the previous section, with the danger of trauma on the side of the head, there is a possibility of injuring the arteria meningea media (middle meningeal artery) where arterial bleeding can occur and which, if untreated, can result in death, which is why we concentrate on covering this area. It is located halfway between the upper edge of the ear and the upper edge of the eye socket where the os frontale, os parietale, and the os sphenoidale meet (this region is called the pterion – see the illustration in the section on the "Skull"). Because the bones at this point are especially thin and the skull has a flat structure here (making it mechanically weak), a fracture is quite possible.

Attack: Punches (be careful not to damage your own hand; it is best to use the ball of the hand, a hammer strike, or the elbow), kicks.

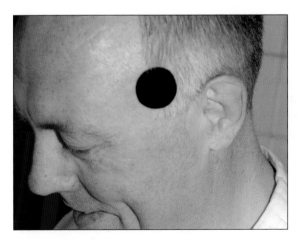

Target mark.

Effects: Skull fractures and traumatic brain injury (unconsciousness, coma, long-lasting brain damage, death) (see more details in the section on the "Skull").

Comments on use:
See previous section.

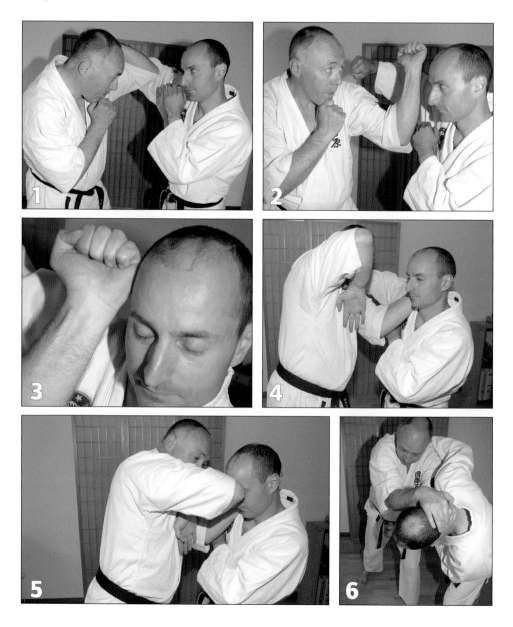

1   The attacker's swinging punch is made ineffective by shortening the distance of reach and cover.

2   The covering arm is used as a hammer fist directly to the temple.

4   Controlling the neck and bringing back the elbow to strike.

6   The hand of the attacking arm grabs hold around the back of the neck. A 90° turn brings the defender into the starting position for a knee kick and puts the attacker off balance.

NOTE: The combination must be executed with constant forward pressure in order to be successful.

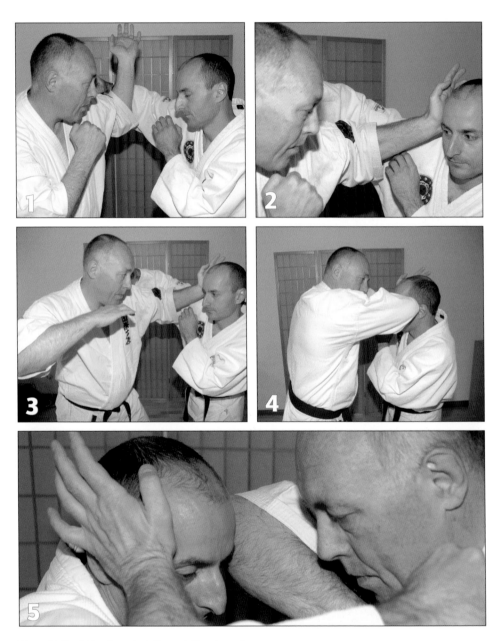

2 Ball of the hand strikes at the temple.
5 'Sandwich' – the attacker's head is between the ball of the hand and the elbow.

1.16   Forehead humps/Tubera frontalia

Center bony section of the forehead (os frontale) to the left and right above the eyebrows; see the section on the "Skull").

Attack: Strike using the knuckles (repeatedly).

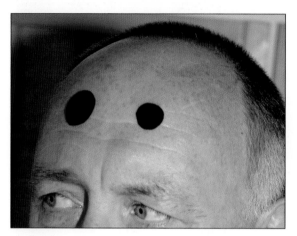

Target mark.

Effects: Pain (skin membrane, or periosteum), possibly from the nervus supraorbitalis or nervus supratrochlearis). After a massive blow, a fracture of the sinus bone may occur (but not after a blow with the knuckles). After a massive blow, the concussion vibration can cause a traumatic brain injury. See the section on the "Skull" for more detail.

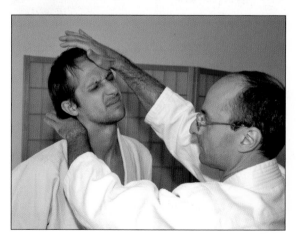

A strike with the ball of the hand, with a simultaneous strike with the edge of the hand at the muscle on the side of the spine of the neck, can have a strong effect, including unconsciousness due to vibration in the brain.

Comments on use:
Freeing techniques (followed by further techniques or running away).

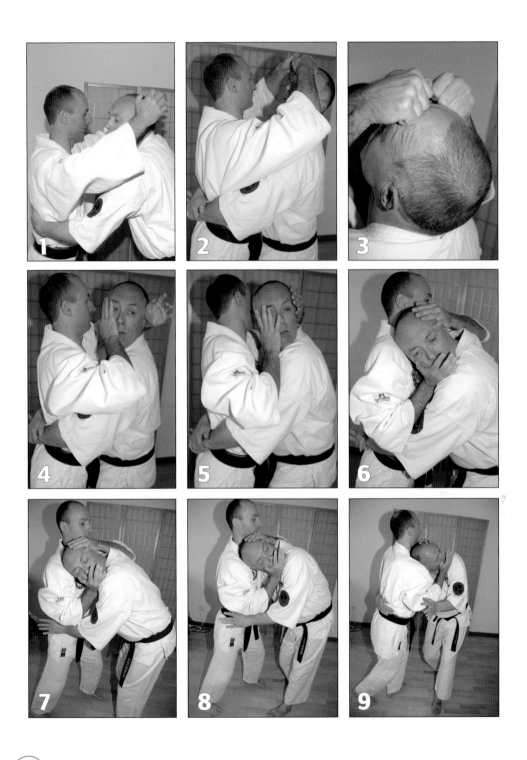

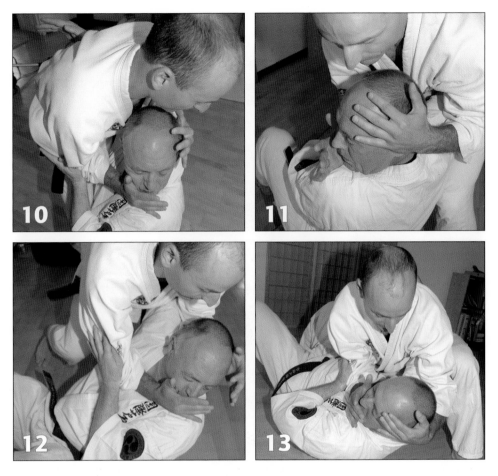

1   Attempt to be grabbed around the waist under the arms.

2   Use a shock technique with a knuckle strike at the bumps on the forehead.

4   Start of the neck lever.

6   The attacker's head is pinned onto the defender's shoulder.

10 The defender executes a Tai-Sabaki rotation while at the same time twisting the opponent's head around.

1.17   Lower jaw

For an illustration see the sections on the "Skull" and "Nervus frontalis."

Attack: Punch. In order to lessen the danger, use the ball of the hand (or base of the fist) or elbow.

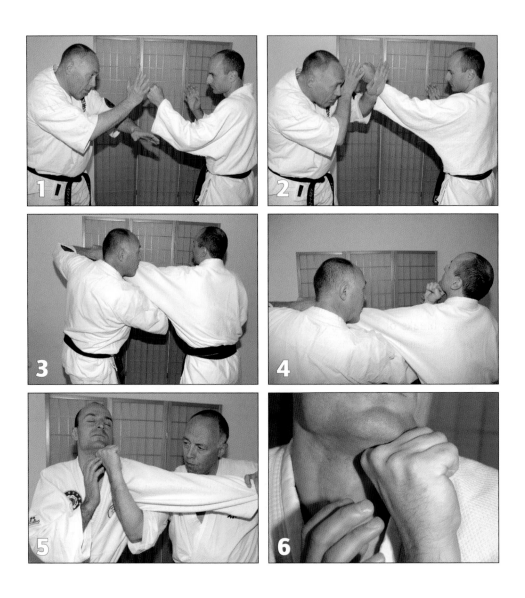

1   The start of the attack is diverted by using a step-in movement. That is to say, the right hand makes contact with the attacking arm and changes the direction of the attack. The left hand grabs hold of the attacking arm.

3   By using a counter movement directly under the attacking arm, an uppercut punch is delivered to the chin.

5   From another viewpoint.

Results: Lip and tongue damage are relatively harmless results. Other injuries depend on the angle at which the blow was delivered (and of course its strength). A horizontal angle is more likely to cause a dislocation or break of the joint of the jaw (especially if the jaw is open at the time) and possibly damage to the teeth. Additionally, a lesion of the nervus auriculotemporalis (see the illustration in the section on the "Nervus frontalis") can occur with resulting paralysis or weakening of the masticatory muscle musculus temporalis. An uppercut blow can result in whiplash from the great strain on the spine of the neck as the head is pushed back (see also Chapter 2 on the Nape of the neck). This can also cause damage to the softer parts of the nape of the neck, e.g., muscles, ligaments, spinal discs, the vessel structures, and the spinal cord. Results can include dizziness, stiff neck, feeling dazed, difficulties in hearing and vision, as well as a reduction of peripheral sight. **Traumatic brain injury** is also possible (see the section on the "Skull").

In serious breaks of the lower jaw, the floor of the mouth becomes instable with a danger of the air passages being blocked due to the position of the base of the tongue.

Partial facial paralysis is also possible, because the nervus facialis is situated forward underneath the parotid gland up to the surface at the rear edge of the lower jaw. Here it lies directly under the skin where it has little protection and thus is easily damaged by external effects.

Comments on use:
This is a classic target for professional fighters, as well as the "not-so-professional" ones; the teeth represent a considerable risk to the striking hand if unprotected.

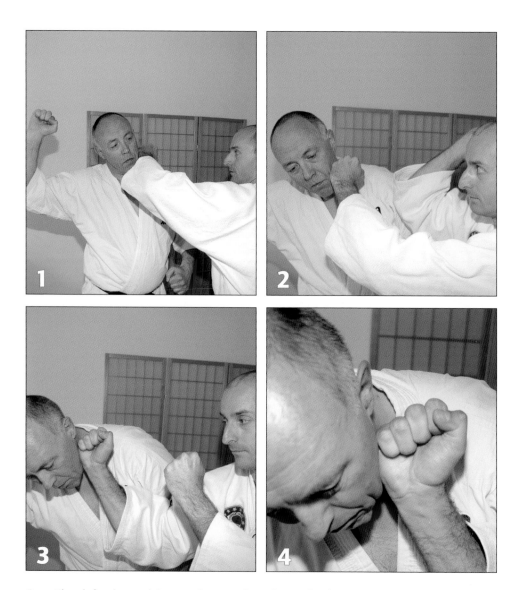

1   The defender anticipates the attack and attacks the attacker's lower jaw with a hammer fist punch.

2   The strike forces the head around...

3   .....followed up with another hammer fist punch.

4   Close-up.

1.18 Submandibular gland/Glandula submandibularis

See the illustration in the section on the "Parotid gland."

The submandibular gland can be felt – right and left – on the mandible angle of the lower jaw between the jaw bone and the musculus digastricus in the so-called submandibular triangle. The submandibular gland is innervated by the nervus facialis and nervus lingualis.

Attack: Punch/pressure using the finger tips/thumbs.

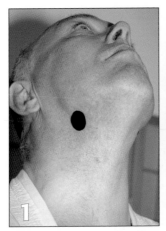 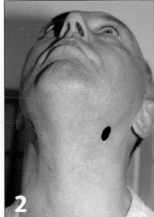 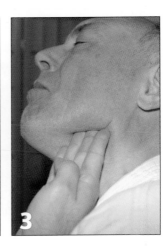

1-2 Target mark.
3 Use the fingers as a spear.

Effects: Nerve pain (neuralgia) can be felt after pressure is applied (see the statements in the Introduction). A lesion of the glandular is possible. There is also a possibility of whiplash resulting from the punch, with similar results as those described earlier.

Comments on use:
Like all nerve points, the degree of sensitivity and effectiveness is individually different.

Uses:

1   The defender anticipates the planned attack by pinning the attacking arm and using the fingers to stab the gland.
2   The attacker leans forward.
3   Close-up.
4   By steering the head, the attacker's punch lands in empty air.
5   Start of the arm lever.
6   Executing the arm lever.
8   The arm is pinned and under control.

Simultaneous use of a pull on the neck and stabbing with the fingers.

 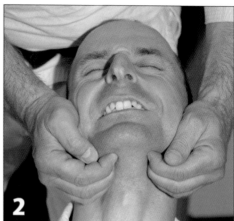

1 Controlling technique when the opponent is on the ground.
2 Close-up.

1+2 Defending one's self against being grabbed around the waist by controlling the head.
2 The defender then hooks his fingers under the attacker's lower jaw and brings him down to the ground.

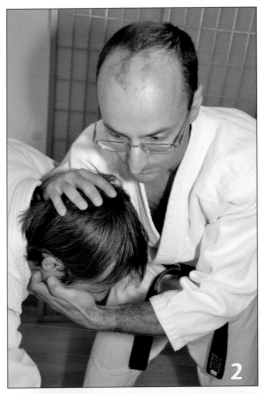

1.19 Lower lip

Attack: Using a pincer grip (with the thumb under the chin), the lower lip is pressed against the incisor teeth; biting the fingers is not possible. The nervus mentalis innervates the lower lip.

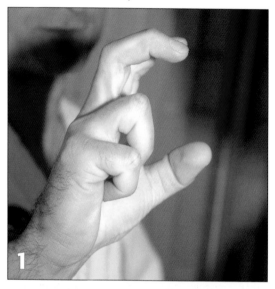

1 How to form the grip.

2 When using the grip, the lower lip is pushed up over the incisors, thus being bitten is not possible.

3 From another viewpoint.

4 Preparing for an O-Soto-Gari.

Effects: Pain (from the pain receptors of the muscles and the mucous membranes).

Comments on use:
Its practical use is clearly limited (being in a position to start the move is the most difficult part).

1.20 Sublingual gland/Glandula sublingualis

For an illustration, see the section on the "Parotid gland."

As the name indicates, the gland lies underneath the tongue – it is the smallest of the 3 pairs of major salivary glands.

Attack: Using a pincer grip (with the thumb under the chin), the forefinger and middle fingers press down on the base of the mouth. Its practical use is clearly limited.

Effects: Pain.

Comments on use:
Like all nerve points, the degree of sensitivity and effectiveness is individually different. Its practical use is clearly limited (being in a position to start the movement is the most difficult part).

1.21   Cheeks

Attack: Using a pincer grip, the flesh of the cheeks is pressed against the upper and lower rows of teeth. The nervus buccalis (see its section) innervates the cheeks.

 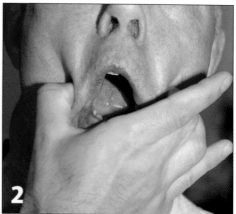

Effects: Pain, the jaws open (dog owners know this technique).

Comments on use:
A counter hold with the hand is necessary (on the neck, chest/lumbar spine region).

1.22   Dental alveoli

The hollows or sockets in the chin bone are called alveoli and the teeth (and roots) are held in place in these. Dental alveoli are present in both the upper jaw bone and the lower jaw bone. The dental alveoli in the lower jaw bone are innervated by the nervus alveolaris, and the nervus infraorbitalis innervates the dental alveoli in the upper jaw bone.

Attack: Jab with the tips of the fingers, knuckle punch.

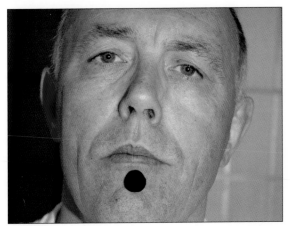

Target mark.

Effects: Pain.

Comments on use:
Freeing techniques (then use follow-up techniques or run away).

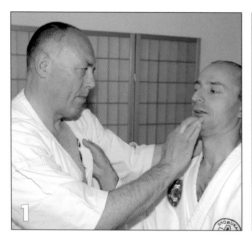 

1   The tips of the fingers press into the dental alveoli. Counter pressure at the back of the neck.

2   Another technique: Use the middle knuckle in a punch.

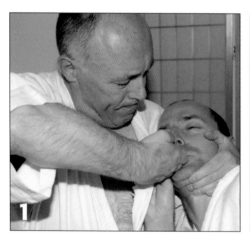 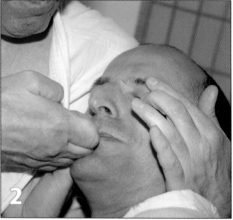

1   Hiraken against the teeth alveoli with a counter hold at the back of the neck.

2   Extension of the previous technique by pressing the middle finger into the opponent's eye.

2 Attack points on the neck

2.1 Carotis/Common carotid artery

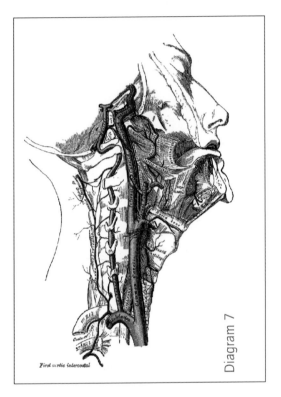

Diagram 7

The carotid artery is on the left and right hand side of the windpipe and the esophagus and is covered only by the neck side muscle and skin. In the region of the neck, one can measure the pulse easily. In the region of the larynx, it divides into the arteria carotis interna and arteria carotis externa. One of the most important points of measuring blood pressure (glomus caroticum) is at this fork in the arteries. This fork is necessary so that when there is a sudden increase of blood pressure the vessels do not break and lead to bleeding. When the blood pressure increases, the internal wall of the carotid sinus stretches, which is registered by the glomus caroticum and transmitted to the brain by the nervous system.

Attack: Strike with either the inside or outside of the hand (also in strangling attacks).

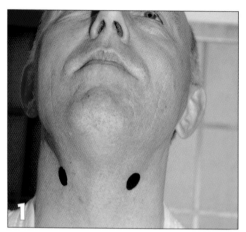 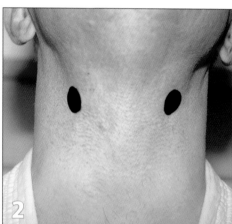

1-2 Target mark.

Effects: The heightened blood pressure stimulates the brain causing the blood vessels to enlarge immediately, specially in the veins of the stomach region – unconsciousness is possible due to the lack of blood supply to the brain. If lying horizontally, the blood flows back into the brain and one will awaken.

In addition, the heart can slow down and be weakened. There is also a lower rate of breathing, which can eventually even come to a full stop. There is a danger of heart attack.[10]

Further injuries can result from any fall.

There is also the danger that plaques can loosen on the internal sides of the carotid artery, move along through the system and cause a stroke in the brain. Such plaques as these are especially found in the fork of the common carotid artery. The danger is higher with increasing age.

As already pointed out in the Introduction, regarding the impact on Uke, one can be irresponsible and be equally juristically dubious when you see this point in the various training videos misused as "evidence" that Kyusho is effective. It can be a particularly delicate subject if there are injuries where the effects are more serious than those planned.

Comments on use:
Suitable for use as Atemi, as well as strangling techniques. In certain instances, danger exists due to the closeness to the larynx.

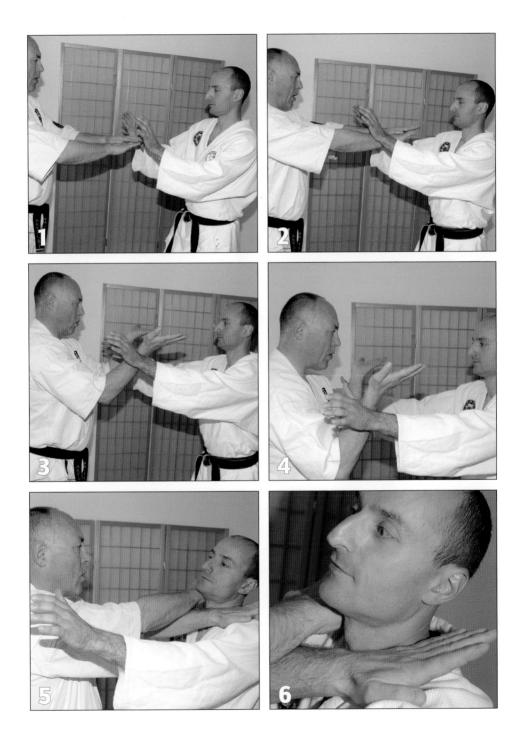

1   The opponent tries to grab hold.
2   The defender moves forward holding his arms in a wedge 'V' shape.
3   The attack is deflected to the outside.
4   The attacker slides past the outside of the defender.
5   Pincer attack using the edge of the hands at the carotid arteries.
6   Close-up.
7   In order to bolster the technique, the attacker's foot is pinned down by standing on it.
8   Close-up.
9   Continue the attack by rattling the sides of the hands against the target.

Additional sequences:

2   Attack using a straight kick with the foot.

3   The kick is swept away by the left arm.

4   The defensive action causes the attacker's kick to be extended.

5   The circular sweeping motion in the counterattack is moved to the use of the inner edge of the hand.

7   Counterattack with the inside edge of the hand and control of the elbow joint at the same time.

The strike can also be executed using the outside edge of the hand (Shuto).

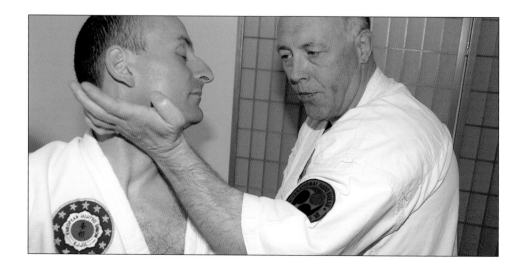

2.2   Nape of the neck/Cervical spine

Consists of the seven vertebrae (C1-C7) between the head and the thoracic spine and is supported by the neck and back muscles as well as several other vertebrae.

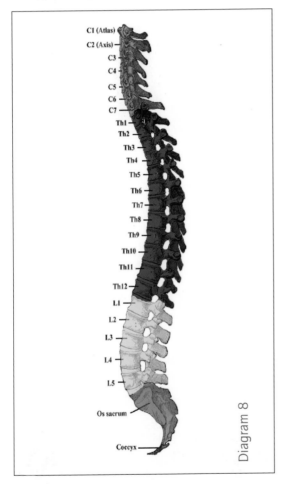

Diagram 8

Attack: Neck lever, punch.

In a rotating neck lever, it is crucial that a combination of stretching the neck and the rotation of the head is applied in order to achieve the optimum effect.

89

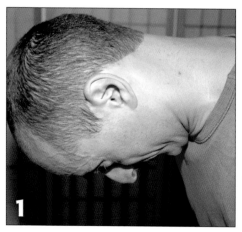
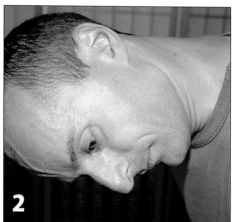

1   Demonstrating the stretching of the neck.
2   Stretching the neck + rotation of the head.

Use in the standing position

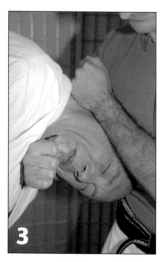

1   Start of the neck lever in a standing position. Notice the beginning of twisting the head and pinning it.
2   No possibility of escape.

When used in groundwork:

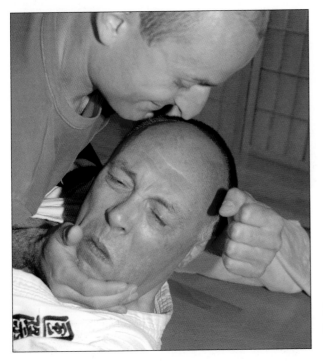

Stefan is pleased with his successful lever of the neck.

Groundwork sequence:

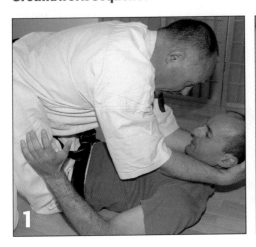

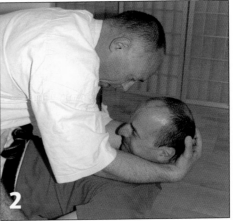

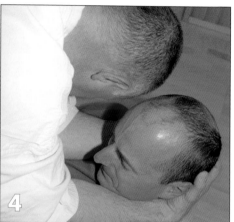

1   The back of the opponent's head is grasped in the flat of the hands. In the clinch, the hands are folded over each other. (Careful! Never link the hands together otherwise there is the danger of breaking the fingers).
2   Stretching the neck.
3   Starting the rotation.

Attack: Strike (edge of the hand, lower arm).

1   Starting position.
2   The right-handed punch is warded off. The right hand is ready for the strike with the edge of the hand that follows.

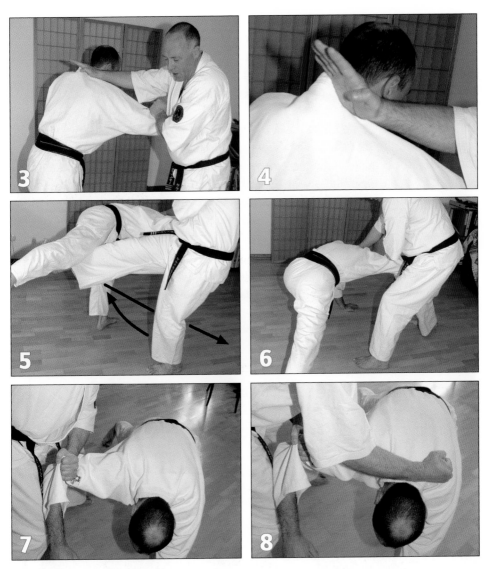

3   Strike with the edge of the hand....

4   ..... and directly grab around the neck.

5   Inside low kick (Uchimomo-Geri). The right-hand kicking leg is quickly moved to the rear, and the opponent is brought off balance by pulling him sharply past the defender.

6   Starting position for a further attack at the neck.

7   Pulling back movement while at the same time controlling the elbow.

8   Attack using the ulna part of the lower arm (potentially fatal).

Effects: Eight branches of nerves originate on each side of the cervical spine. The upper four form the cervical plexus and innervate the neck and its muscles as well as the diaphragm. The lower four, together with the nerves of the first thoracic vertebra, form the arm plexus (plexus brachialis) and innervate the chest, back and arm muscles, as well as the skin covering them.

The vertebral arteries are found down the cervical spine and, together with the carotid artery, they ensure that the brain is supplied with blood. Lesions of the spinal marrow (caused by broken bones in the cervical spine) lead to feelings of numbness and paralysis of the legs, arms, torso and, in the case of injury in the higher section (in injuries to the spinal marrow around the region of the fourth vertebra or higher), paralysis of the diaphragm and thus breathing. Moreover, it results in a loss of control over the bladder and bowels, as well as deadening sexual functions. Whiplash is a moderate form of injury to the marrow in the cervical spine and does not damage the vertebrae. It has the typical symptoms of headache, fatigue, dizziness and nausea. Serious forms of whiplash are accompanied with instability in the passage from head to neck. These injuries are those to the ligaments or damage to the joint capsule in the head joint. Symptoms of instabilities in the passage from head to neck are:

- Dizziness
- Drowsiness
- Burning or sharp pain at the back of the head
- Problems with hearing and vision, limited peripheral vision
- Perceptual disorders, attention disorders, disorientation
- Rapid exhaustion
- Insomnia
- Feeling of weakness
- Pain and/or sensation of numbness or tingling on the facial or arm skin (paresthesia)
- Unsteady gait
- Muscle disturbances, such as cramps (spasmodic)

Comments on use:
Targets are easily reached, however the effects are dependent upon the physical constitution of the other person.

The same sequence as above, but for clarity, from another viewpoint.

7   Take control with the right hand. Pull back the left hand for a fresh strike.

2.3   Jugular notch/Fossa jugularis

Location: Lies in a hollow between the two collarbones and bordered below by the upper edge of the breastbone.

Attack: Apply pressure or, with a jab, use the fore and middle fingers thus causing irritation of the windpipe (trachea).

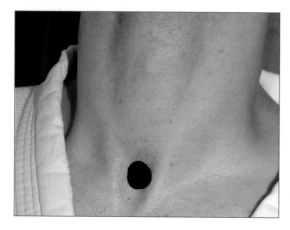

Target mark.

1 This is how to hold the hand for the attack on the jugular notch.

2 Alternative way of holding the hand for delving into and behind the breastbone.

3 Pressure of the fingers is applied diagonally upward (for the best effect).

Example of its use:

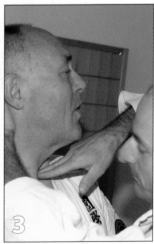

1 The opponent grabs around under the arms.

2 Shock strike with the knuckles against the nervus frontalis (see earlier). The head is pushed back by this...

3 ....and allows the defender to attack the jugular notch with jabbing fingers.

Effects: Pain and irritation of the throat caused by irritation of the tiny hairs (cilia) on the inside of the windpipe. A fracture of the windpipe occurs mainly as a result of a direct break (this specifically affects older persons) of the ossified upper tracheal rings (horseshoe-shaped rings, or cartilages, enclosing the windpipe, open to the rear – see the illustration in the section on the "Larynx") (e.g., caused by a blunt blow); in cases of complete fracture, retract the stumps.

Comments on use:

In short reaches, it may be possible to bring the opponent down to the ground (to do this, the other hand must hold behind the head/neck). Used as a jabbing attack from greater range (precision is required; in certain circumstances, there is danger due to proximity of the larynx). Alternatively, use it as a freeing technique (then do a follow-up technique or run away).

Additional sequences:

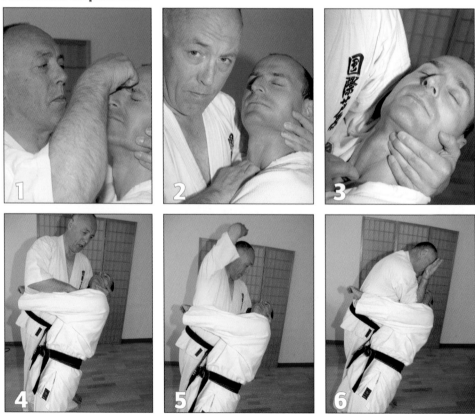

1   Shock technique (as described earlier).
2   Grip the breastbone.
4   Attacker is brought down to his knees.
6   Concluding technique using the elbow (potentially fatal).

Parts of the sequence for clarity:

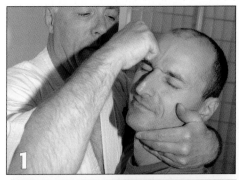
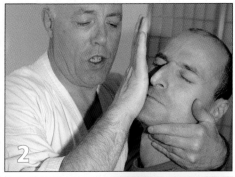
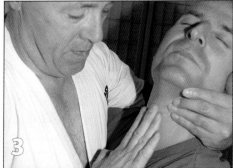
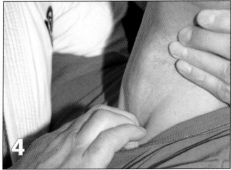

1   Repeat use of the shock technique.
2   Contact is maintained with the opponent's face. The hand slips toward the throat.
4   Grabbing into the hollow.
5   Defensive strike with the tips of the fingers diagonally upward (careful of the larynx!).

The most reliable strike – upward and diagonal – is the one that uses the whole hand because one of the fingers will always find its target.

2.4   Neck side muscle/Musculus sternocleidomastoideus

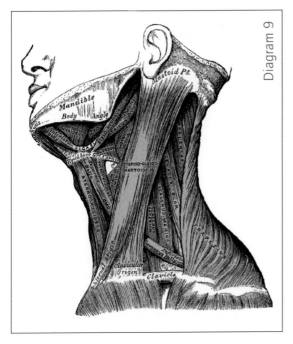

Diagram 9

Origin: Front surface of the breastbone and inside part of the collarbone.

Insertion: Processus mastoideus (mastoid process) of the temporal bone (behind the ear).

The function of this muscle is to rotate the head to the opposite side or obliquely rotate the head. It also flexes the neck. The sternocleidomastoid is innervated by the ipsilateral accessory nerve.

Attack: Pincer grip with the fingers on the center of the belly of muscle or hook the fingers into it.

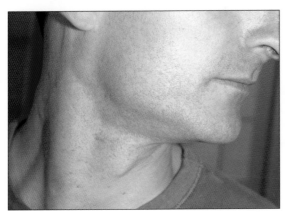

Illustration of the bundle of muscles.

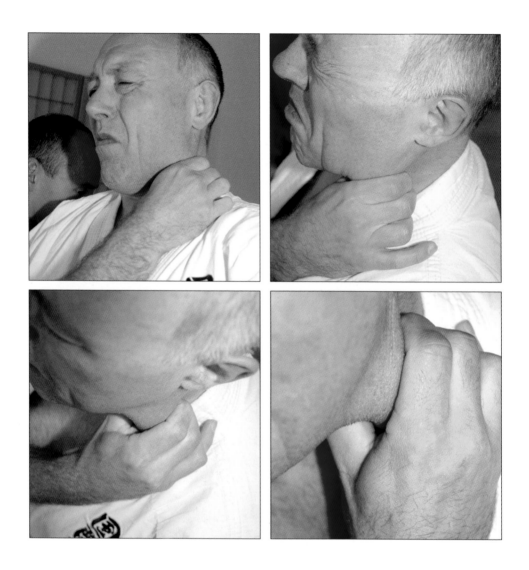

Effects: Muscle pain; be careful with pressure on the carotid (see its section).

Comments on use:
When at short range, the opponent can be easily steered.

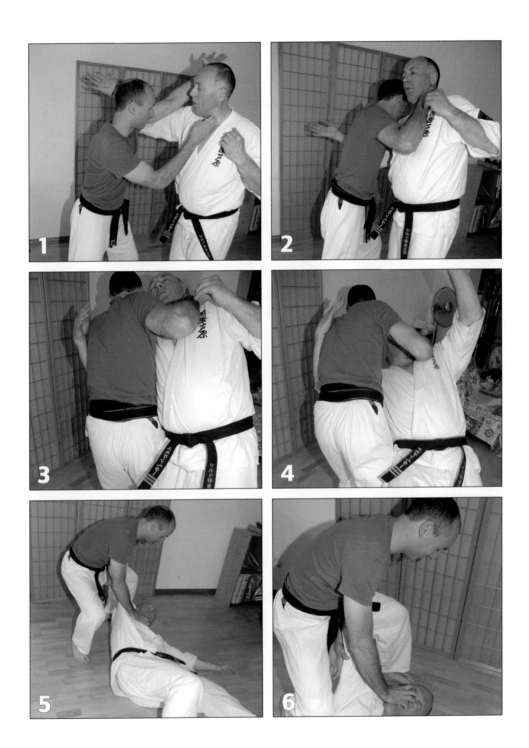

1 The punch at the ear is deflected.
2 Starting the throw.
3 O-Soto-Gari.
6 Concluding technique: jabbing into the eye.

Variation: Controlling from behind.

  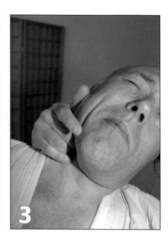

1 Grab hold of the muscle while controlling with the other arm.

2.5   Neck side muscle – insertion point

Insertion point of the musculus sternocleidomastoideus is at the mastoid process (processus mastoideus) of the temporal bone (behind the ear).

Attack: Strike with the outside edge of the hand, inside edge of the hand, ulna or base of the fist.

 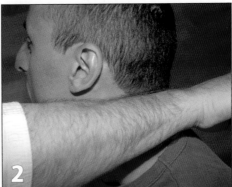

1   Attack using the lower arm (bony part: spoke bone = radius).
2   Close-up.

Effects: When contracting on the one side, the neck side muscle brings the head in the direction of the shoulder. Together with the stretch reflex (see Introduction), the head or brain is concussed and results possibly in short periods of disorientation. When a massive blow is felt, there is a possibility of injury to the cervical spine (see its section).

Comments on use:
A wide spectrum of uses is available, e.g., in support of a throw such as O-Soto-Gari or also used as a shock technique.

After blocking, grab around the body by pushing the attacker's head. Then strike using the edge of the hand against the insertion point of the neck side muscle.

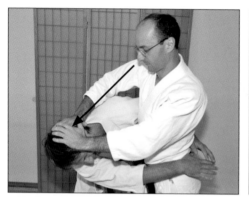 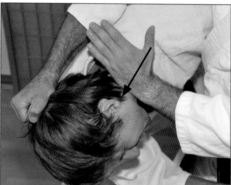

Free yourself from the clinch by applying pressure to the nervus auricularis magnus, use the same hand to deliver a strike with the base of the fist against the insertion point of the neck side muscle.

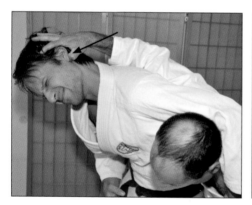 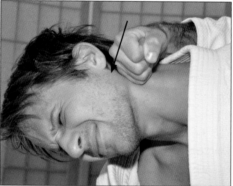

2.6　Neck side muscle – insertion point hollow

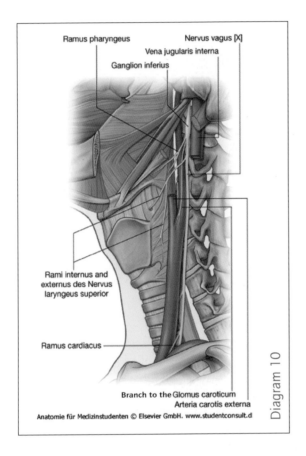

The hollow formed by the left and right neck side muscles (musculus sternocleido mastoideus) between the collarbone and the start of the breastbone; just above the collarbone (see the illustration in the section for the "Neck side muscle"). "Insertion" means the site of attachment of the muscle to the bone it moves.

The nervus vagus runs through the neck down to the body in the same sheath as the arteria carotis communis. Here it innervates the heart, the bronchia, the digestive tract and the ureter (to reach this, the pressure must be very strong). Regardless, the effect is felt by the pain caused by pressure on the origin of the muscle.

Attack: Thumb presses diagonally downward toward the middle.

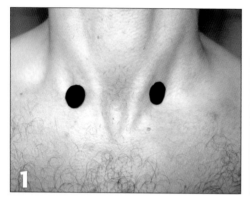 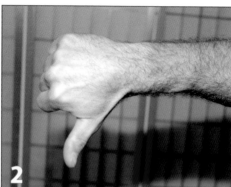

1   Target mark.
2   How the thumb should be held.

Effects: Nerve pain (neuralgia) can be felt after pressure applied (compare the statements in the Introduction). When pressure is applied on the arteria carotis communis, there is a temporary reduction of blood supply to the brain resulting in dizziness. The windpipe can also become irritated.

Comments on use:
Good technique for short range work: finding the correct spot requires practice before one can expect a high degree of success.

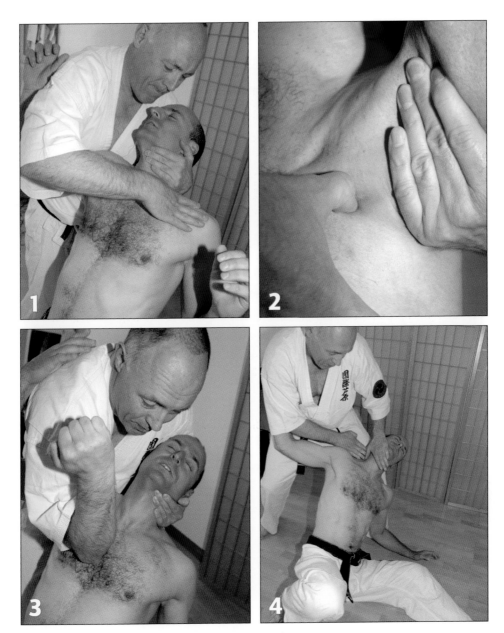

1 Controlling the head + attack using the thumb.
2 Close-up.
3 Elbow into the breastbone.
4 Head is pinned for the concluding technique.

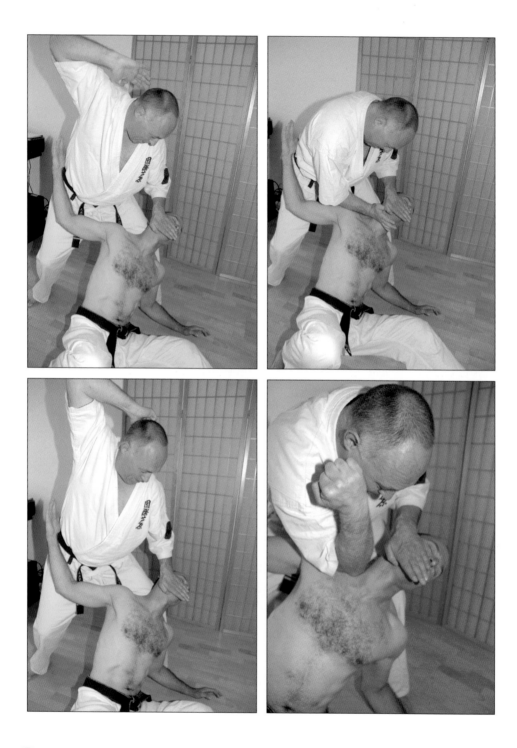

2.7   Larynx

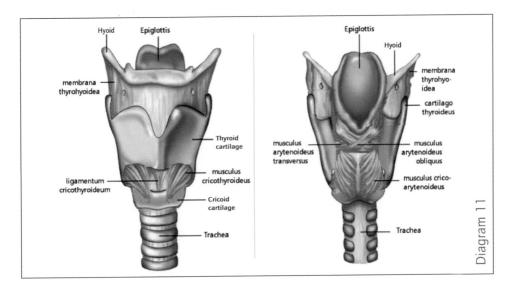

Diagram 11

This target area is very much at risk because the area has no natural protection. The larynx consists of the tongue, as well as three cartilages – the thyroid cartilage, the cricoid cartilage, and the epiglottis. In addition, there are two arytenoids cartilages. The cartilages are held together by membranes.

Attack: Strikes using the inside or outside edge of the hand, the flat of the hand, fist, knuckles or being gripped.

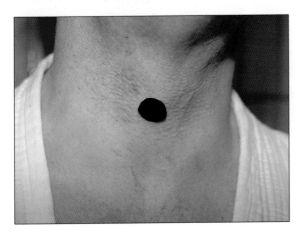

Target mark.

111

Effects: If the larynx collapses, there is an acute danger of suffocation because the airways become obstructed. Counter-measures: Tracheotomy (or coniotomy dependent upon location). There is a further possibility of a spasm of the vocal cords with closure of the glottis and possible swelling of the epiglottis. If the hyoid is broken, there will be breathing and speech problems caused by the contortion of the muscles surrounding it.

Comments on use:
Regarding effectiveness and accessibility, this target is almost on the same level as the eyes.

 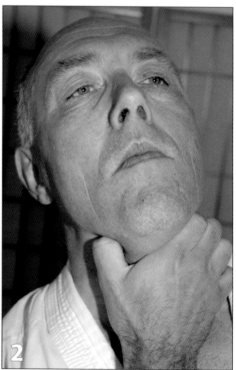

1 An effective weapon is to use the fork formed by the open thumb and first finger to strike or seize the throat (Japanese: "Toho"). Following a successful strike, the attack can be followed up by grabbing or squeezing the larynx.

2.8 Clavicle hollow

Attack: Thumb pressure – directed at the plexus cervicalis (cervical plexus) and the musculi scaleni (scalene muscles) (see the illustration in the section on "Neck side muscle").

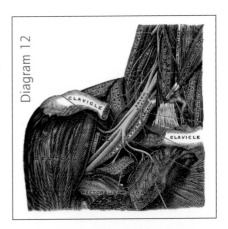

Diagram 12

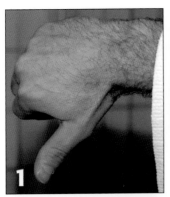
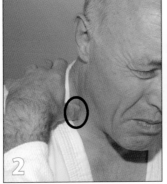
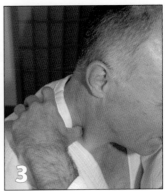

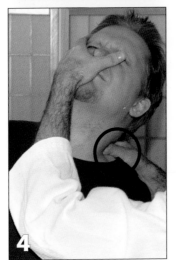

1 How to hold the thumb for the attack. 2 Target mark. 3 From another viewpoint. 4 The pressure of the thumb on the plexus cervicalis can be supported by using a neck lever.

Effects: Nerve pain (neuralgia) can be felt after pressure is applied (see the statements in the Introduction).

Comments on use:
Good technique for short range work; finding the correct spot requires practice before one can expect a high degree of success.

2.9   Trapezius/Musculus trapezius

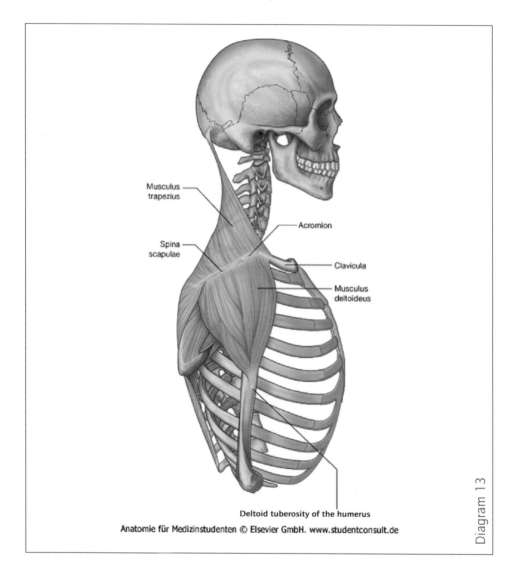

Deltoid tuberosity of the humerus

Anatomie für Medizinstudenten © Elsevier GmbH. www.studentconsult.de

Diagram 13

Attack: Strike (with the edge of the hand, hammer fist, strike using the lower arm [ulna]) against the musculus trapezius where it connects with the neck; pincer grip on the belly of its muscle.

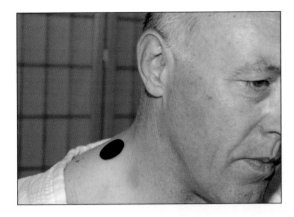

Target mark.

Effects: Muscle pain; together with the stretching reflex (see Introduction), the head or brain is concussed (this means that the strike is at the lower base of the skull).

For the possible effects on the trapezius muscle, see the section on the "Biceps."

Comments on use:
Whiplash is possible with the results already explained several times earlier. This is possibly a difficult target to reach in unfavorable conditions; the strike must be delivered with force.

1   Warding off the swinging punch.
2   Grab hold of the opponent's clothing while at the same time delivering a kick to the inside of the knee.
3   Pull back the arm to deliver the strike at the trapezius.

4 Execute the strike by hitting with the ulna.
5 Grab hold and control the neck.
6 Concluding technique with a knee kick.

1 Pull back the arm.
2 Strike diagonally downward with the radius.
3 Close-up.

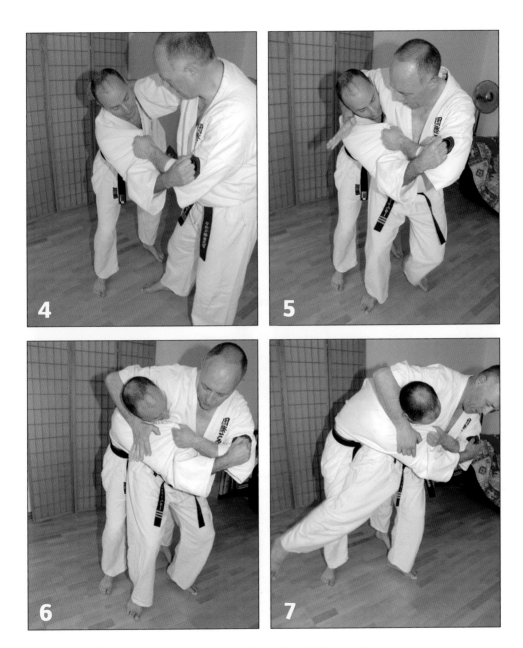

4 The strike changes over into a hip throw (Koshi Guruma).

5 Movement to create the pivot.

7 To increase the effect of the throw, the opponent's right leg is swept away.

3 Attack points on the torso

3.1 Armpit/Axilla

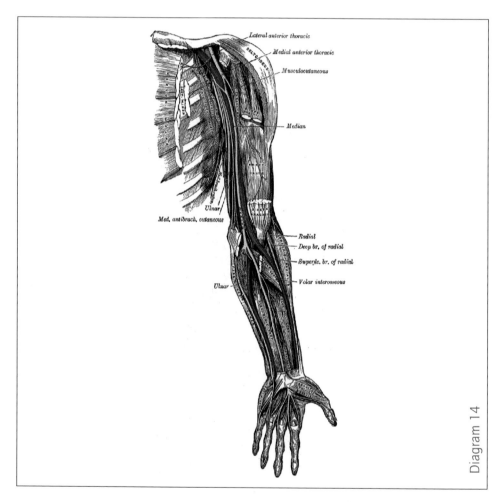

Lateral anterior thoracic

Medial anterior thoracic

Musculocutaneous

Median

Ulnar

Med. antibrach. cutaneous

Radial

Deep br. of radial

Superfic. br. of radial

Volar interosseous

Ulnar

Diagram 14

The armpit is the area on the human body directly under the joint where the arm connects to the shoulder and is bordered by the chest muscle in the front, at the rear by the back muscle, and on the inside by the rib cage. It lies under the skin. The extensions of the plexus brachialis, namely the nervus medianus, nervus ulnaris, and nervus radialis can be found in the armpit. These nerves run through the whole of the upper extremities.

Attack: Kick, jab with the fingers.

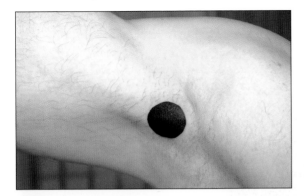

Target mark.

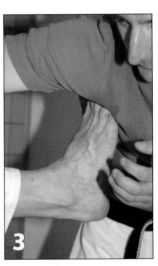

1   The opponent is forced to guard himself by applying a lever to his arm. This makes the armpit vulnerable....
2   .....so that a kick can be delivered.
3   Close-up.

Effects: Nerve pain/neuralgia (see statements in the Introduction).

Comments on use:
Like all nerve points, the degree of sensitivity, as well as the effect achieved is individually different; the armpit is relatively seldom exposed, and moreover, as with all targets on the torso, often well protected by clothing.

3.2   Breastbone/Sternum

See also the illustration in the section on the "Ribs."

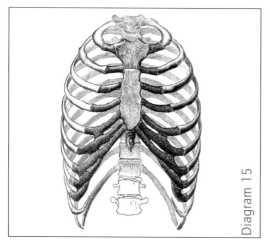

Diagram 15

Part of the rib cage (Latin: thorax).

Attack: Strike using the knuckles of the fingers, head butt, kick with the knee, base of the fist.

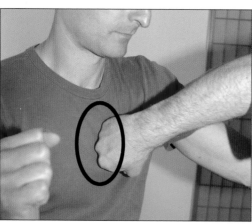

Target mark.

Effects: Pain, tickle cough in the throat, fracture of the bone, passing out/fainting, breathing difficulties, shock effect to the heart leading to possible cardiac arrest, death.

It is possible that it will have an effect on the heart. However, this procedure is used in heart massage where pressure is applied to the chest cage. Sometimes, in an emergency, a thump with the base of the fist is done to the chest (just left of the central line) in order to resuscitate the correct heartbeat in cases of ventricular fibrillation.

A state of "commotio cordis" (heart vibration) can be caused even with little force. A U.S. study on this[11], in which 128 cases were reviewed, reported that in most instances baseballs, footballs or other balls were involved. According to the study, there was a window of 15 milliseconds when the risk was at its greatest – the blow had to be directly above the heart.

There appears to be no particular predisposition for a state of "commotio cordis" – it can strike anyone in unfavorable conditions as described. Younger persons, however, are more at risk as they have a more elastic ribcage than older people. Only 16% of the 128 cases reviewed in the study survived.[12]

Comments on use:
The target is easily accessible; however, like all targets on the torso, the ribcage is protected by clothing (particularly for strikes using the knuckles of the fingers).

1   Punch with the fist.
2   The punch is warded off by swiping it away from the outside to inside.
3   The movement turns into a punch coming in diagonally downward.
4   Conclude with a hook to the liver.

 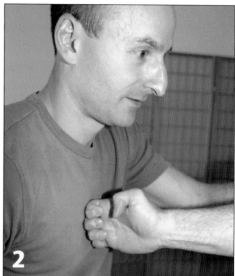

1 Attack using a punch (Hiraken).
2 Close-up.

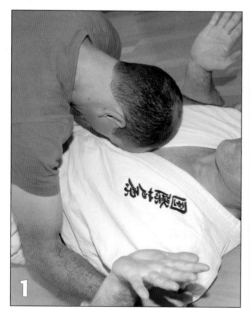 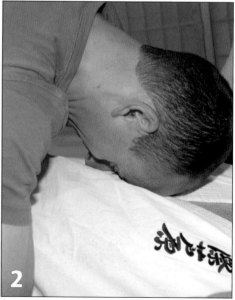

1 Using the head in groundwork.
2 Side view.

 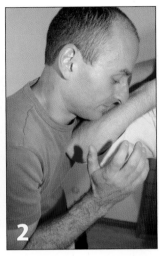 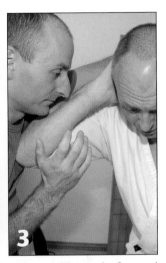

1 The opponent's in-swinging attack is negated by moving deliberately forward while covering the head.

2 The harder the opponent attacks, the more the pressure is transferred to his breastbone.

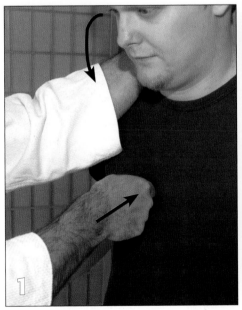 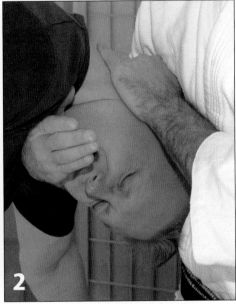

1 By applying pressure with the knuckles of the fingers (a rubbing motion is also possible) and pulling the back of his head forward, the opponent is forced to lean forward – in this case into a neck lever.

123

3.3   Chest muscles

The "musculus pectoralis major" (large chest muscle) covers the whole of the frontal rib area. The muscle fibers overlap at the arm: The fibers that come upward join the upper arm further up than the fibers that come from the collarbone. They create an archway where the foremost limitation forms the armpit. The large chest muscle is innervated by the nervus pectoralis lateralis and the nervus pectoralis medialis.

Attack: Grip the armpit between the fingers of the hand.

  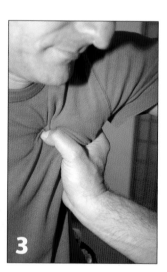

1   Grab hold as a defense against the attempt to take hold of the shoulder.
2   The defense is successful by using a pincer grip with the hand to locate the chest muscle.
3   Close-up.

Effects: Pain.

Comments on use:
It is necessary to push the opponent backwards; a harmless technique.

Possible difficulty when faced by thick-muscled or corpulent persons, as well as anyone wearing thick clothing.

3.4 Nipples/Mammary glands/Glandula mammaria

The vessel supply and the nerval innervation of the male nipple are similar to a smaller degree to those of the female glands.

The sensitive innervation of the mammary glands comes from the branches of the intercostal nerves (nervi intercostales) that run as medial and lateral mammary branches to their supply area.

Attack: Biting or pinching (pincer grip).

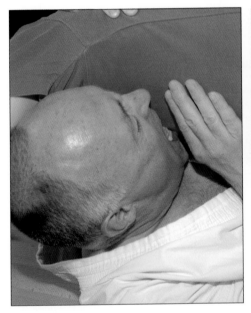 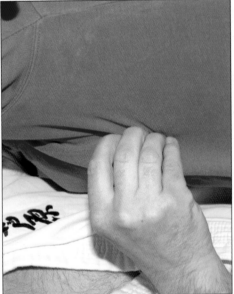

Effects: Pain.

Comments on use:
Usually well covered or protected by clothing.

3.5   Testicles

Attack: Kick (with the foot or knee), punch, grip.

Example of defense

Effects: The main sensitivity of the testicles to pain comes from the sensitive nerve fibers (branches of the nervus genitofemoralis) of the scrotum.

Because the genitals are also innervated by the parasympathetic nerve system, it can – as always, when this nerve system is involved – lead to a lowering of the blood pressure or to a slowing down of the heartbeat and breathing. Possible results of these effects are more likely to include vomiting, unconsciousness and cardiac arrest.[13]

In cases of blunt traumas, there is a danger of damaging the supplying arteries and bleeding inside the testicle pouch. Puncture of the testicle pouch can lead to inflammation of the testicles or even abscesses. Because of the open channel of the vaginal process to the abdominal cavity, peritonitis can occur.

Therefore, using significant force in this area can cause permanent infertility.

A kick in this area can cause the displacement of the testicles into the abdominal cavity, accompanied by stark pain. It is also possible that the pubic bone may be damaged (see section 3.17).

Dull pain and a small bruise can be signs of a harmless contusion of the testicles. Pronounced bruising and lots of pain, possibly accompanied by nausea, are signs of a more serious injury. Above all, after an injury when the testicles cannot be individually felt, a visit to the urologist is necessary.

Comments on use:
This region is always instinctively protected, while follow-up actions are possible, even if the target is not hit.

 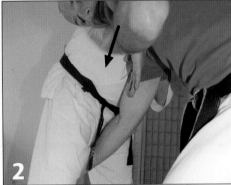

1   Attempted neck lever.
2   Defend by delivering a strike with the lower arm at the testicles.

CAUTION!! Make sure that the opponent's arm around the neck is loose and controlled. This helps the attacker to avoid a situation in which the lower arm strikes the testicles. The opponent's reflex reaction tends to strengthen his grip around the neck.

 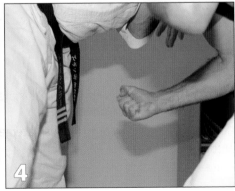

3   Close-up of the strike.
4   Alternative defense: hook punch at the testicles.

1   Squeezing, twisting, and ripping the testicles is best practiced using an object such as a bunch of rolled-up socks.

1   Starting technique: Kick at the hollow at the back of the knee.
2   Kick at the testicles is executed from behind.
3   Variation: Kick with the toes.

1   A sweeping kick opens up the standing position of the attacker.

2   Start of the sweeping kick. The sweeper's standing leg is well outside the attacker's standing position in order to develop more force.

3   The λ (= distance between feet) is lengthened.

4   Using the sweeping foot, the kick is delivered directly.

5   Alternative: Kick with the other leg.

1   Inside low kick – thus lengthening the λ.
2   Hard to soft.

3.6 Liver

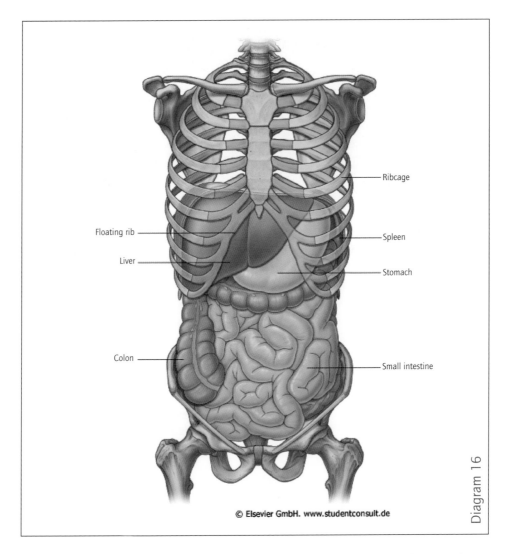

Floating rib

Liver

Colon

Ribcage

Spleen

Stomach

Small intestine

Diagram 16

© Elsevier GmbH. www.studentconsult.de

The liver is located on the right side of the upper abdomen and runs down as far as the bottom right-hand floating rib. It is the central organ of the whole metabolism of the body and the largest gland. The liver is held in a membrane capsule. Only this membrane has a dense network of fine nerves capable of reporting to the brain.

Attack: Kick, punch.

Hook at the liver

Effects: Many of the inner organs, just as it is with the liver, are supplied with large amounts of blood. If it is hit hard, there is the danger of rupturing the liver and hidden internal bleeding. Because of its "hidden" nature, internal bleeding of this sort is insidious. A blunt abdominal trauma of this type can, above all, lead to fatality caused by shock from the high loss of blood from internal bleeding. Other symptoms include pressure pain, nausea, a pallid and wan appearance (because of the shock), dizziness, and vomiting. In general, with such injuries, there is the danger of internal bleeding. This can develop over a period of several days. It is also possible that although the veins do not rupture they may be so badly damaged that when put under renewed exertion (e.g., in sport) spontaneous ruptures may occur, which in turn lead to heavy bleeding. This can also have complications and eventually lead to fatality in the worst cases.

Comments on use:
Possible difficulty when faced by thick-muscled or corpulent persons, as well as anyone wearing thick clothing.

1 The punch attack is warded off using both hands.

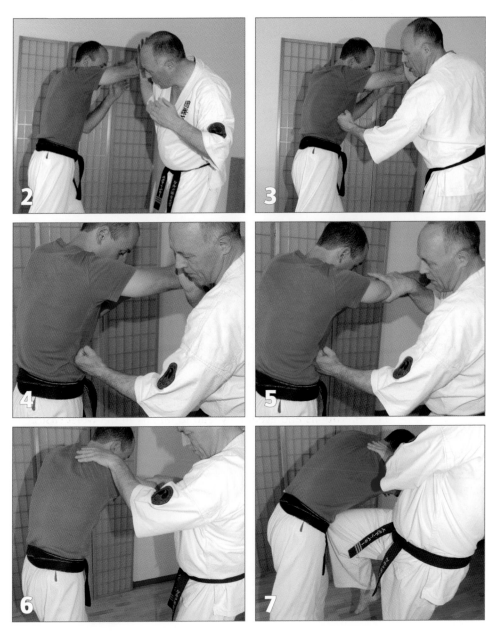

3 Hook at the liver. **4** Close-up. **5** Grab the arm....

6 ...and control the shoulder....

7 ...and transfer the technique over to deliver a knee kick at the liver while, at the same time, pulling with both hands.

133

3.7 Groin

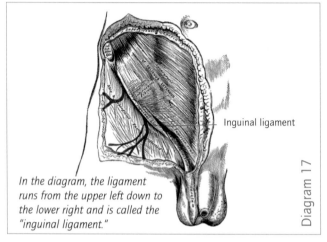

Inguinal ligament

In the diagram, the ligament runs from the upper left down to the lower right and is called the "inguinal ligament."

Diagram 17

Attack: Punch, kick, finger jab.

1 An attempted kick is countered by kicking at the groin.

3 The groin is struck. The kick at the groin must be executed diagonally (left foot against the opponent's left groin and vice versa). If you don't kick diagonally, the opponent can counter by executing a kick at the open side because the opponent's center of gravity will not be affected by the kick.

Effects: Pain, hernia rupture.

The region of the groin, particularly the inguinal canal (canalis inguinalis), is a well-known weak spot. It runs above the inguinal ligament. At this spot, a hernia can occur, which can also occur after heavy bodily strain. The contents of the abdominal cavity (peritoneum) can protrude through the abdominal wall. Pain from this can be low to heavy and convulsive. A hard lump can be felt above the groin. Ruptures are dangerous, above all when the organs of the abdominal cavity (such as the intestine) are trapped in the break. As a result of the this, the trapped intestine swells still further, and is therefore cut off from the blood supply. This is known as strangulation and can lead to necrosis of the trapped part of the organ. In addition, an ileus (obstruction of the bowels) can occur. Both situations are life-threatening and require immediate operative surgical attention. In certain cases, a resection (partial removal of an organ) is necessary.

Comments on use:
This causes a probable bending over at the hips, which opens the possibility for follow-up actions.

The groin is a good target to put the opponent off balance, especially when he has a well-padded torso.

A kick in the groin from a clinch. **IMPORTANT!** The opponent's right arm must be pinned down otherwise he can grab the attacking leg and cause the defender to fall.

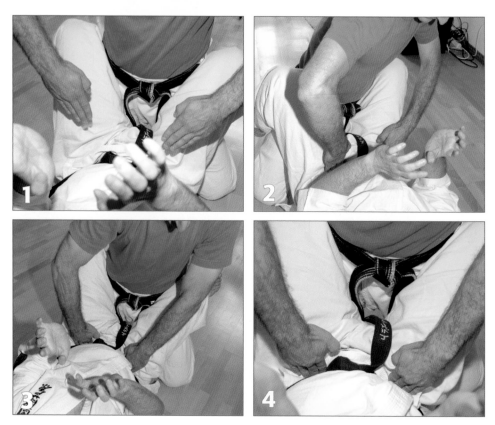

1 How to hold the hands when jabbing with the fingers at the groin.
3 From another viewpoint.

3.8 Stomach

For an illustration, see the section on the "Liver."

Attack: Punch, kick.

1 Clinch situation.

2-6 Series of knee kicks at the stomach area.

Effects: Pain, perforation of the stomach.

The wall of the stomach can rupture following a blunt blow, which means its contents will empty into the abdominal cavity. Sudden severe pains accompanied by vomiting, tension in the abdominal wall, and symptoms of shock begin.

Rupture of the stomach wall must always be considered an emergency, because, if untreated, it can be fatal. The main danger of perforation of the stomach is peritonitis with subsequent blood poisoning (sepsis) caused by the escape of the stomach contents into the abdominal cavity. The danger is greater if the stomach is full.

Comments on use:
Possible difficulty when faced by thick-muscled or corpulent persons, as well as anyone wearing thick clothing.

3.9   Spleen

See the illustration in the section on the "Liver."

In humans, the spleen is a fist-sized organ that lies below the eighth and ninth rib on the left-hand side of the upper abdomen beneath the diaphragm and above the left kidney. This organ holds a large quantity of blood.

Attack: Punch, kick, knee kick.

1   Hook punch at the spleen.
2   Close-up.
3   The attacker's arm is then controlled.
4   Further attack at the spleen using the elbow.

Effects: If the ribs on the left side are injured, there is a possibility that the spleen can rupture (in some instances, appears as pain in the upper abdomen) which means it may bleed into the abdominal cavity, which of course is not visible on the outside. The spleen capsule can control the bleeding for a short period, which is why the first symptoms appear after a few days.

Hypovolemic shock of this kind (also shock from lack of blood volume) comes about by an insufficient intravascular level of blood (in the blood vessels). Results are often unconsciousness, as well as cessation of breathing and cardiac arrest. Loss of about 50% of blood is almost always fatal without medical attention.

If shock is not treated over a longer period of time, irreversible shock can set in and there is the danger of a failure of the kidneys and a fatal multiple organ failure.

Comments on use:
Possible difficulty when faced by thick-muscled or corpulent persons, as well as anyone wearing thick clothing.

1   A further example: Knee kick at the spleen.
2   Close-up.

3.10   Deltoid muscles

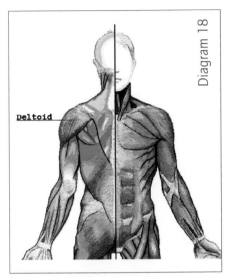

Diagram 18

See also the illustrations in the sections on the "Armpit" and "Clavicle/Collar bone."

The musculus deltoideus (deltoid) is a triangular skeletal muscle that lies over the shoulder joint like a parcel and gives it stability by pressing the head joint of the upper arm bone into its socket. Its function is in lifting the upper arm.

Attack: Punch (with the fist, elbow).

Target mark.

Effects: Damage to organs or parts of the body caused by external direct, blunt force without visible injury to the skin is known as **bruising**. This creates an edema (swelling) of the tissues and extravasation of blood from the damaged capillaries in the surrounding tissue and can appear as a bruise. Generally, pain is immediate and limits mobility. In cases of larger swellings, stiffening of the muscle can occur.

Similar events occur in contusions when the body tissue is pressed together.

In a **torn muscle fiber**, the reticular fibers are damaged and local inflammatory symptoms occur. At the same time, local reduction of tonus (state of tension in the muscles) is apparent in the damaged area. With tears in larger muscles, sometimes clear recesses or knotting of the muscles in the affected area can be seen.

Thrombosis is unlikely.

Tears of the fascia skin are hardly likely; however, compartment syndrome can be possible (swelling in the muscle with reduced blood circulation, increase of pressure and, if not treated, possible necrosis).

It is also possible to damage the arm socket and the tendons of the rotator cuff muscles, which form a collar around the whole of the shoulder.

Interference is possible also in the nervus axillaris that originates from the plexus brachialis and innervates the musculus deltoideus.

Comments on use:
The limitations in mobility can be deduced from the statements above. The effect is limited where the muscles are well-developed (fit to fight); a small impact surface increases the effect.

 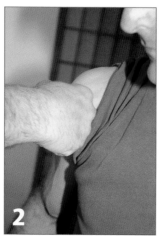 

1   Examples of attacking strikes at the shoulder.... **2** ....with the fist....
3   ....and with the elbow.

1   The strike with the elbow at the rear of the deltoid muscle can be used to twist the opponent around.

2   This disadvantageous position is used by the defender to execute a Hadaka-Jime ("naked strangle").

3   The opponent is brought to his knees.

After successful defense, here the strike at the musculus deltoideus provides further support to turn the opponent around and throw him backwards.

3.11   Kidneys

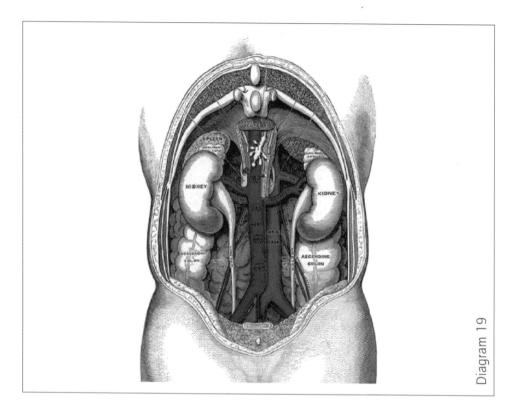

Diagram 19

Location of the kidneys. Dissected view from rear.

The functions of the kidneys are the secretion of superficial waste products produced by metabolism and toxins and washing them from the body through the urinary passage.

Every human has two kidneys that lie left and right of the spine underneath the diaphragm and are protected by a capsule of fat. They are each shaped like a bean and are about 10-12 cm long. Each of the kidneys is protected by a thin, firm capsule of connective tissue round the organ and lies, together with the adrenal glands, bedded in and cushioned in an adipose capsule. They are partially protected by the ribs above them (11th and 12th pairs of ribs).

Attack: Strike (fist, elbow), knee kick.

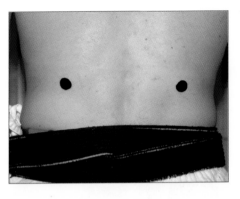

Target mark.

Effects: All forms of damage to the kidneys can be defined as renal trauma. Children are at greater risk due the lack of cushioning fatty tissue to take the shock.

Renal trauma can be divided into contusion or bruising, renal rupture or tear, and complete destruction of the kidney. The predominant symptoms are flank tumor, flank pain, and blood visible in the urine – the latter, however, is not necessarily related to the amount of blood in the urine. If the ureter is completely blocked by blood clots or if the stem vessels are torn off, there may be no blood in the urine at all.

Additional symptoms: Local bruising (hematoma), severe pain, possible leakage of urine from the open wound (caused by knifing or shooting).

Loss of blood from a ruptured kidney can be fatal from shock.

Comments on use:
Possible difficulty when faced by thick-muscled or corpulent persons, as well as anyone wearing thick clothing.

1 The neck lever is supported by delivering a strike with the base of the forefinger knuckle joint of the thumb side of the hand.

1   The step forward by the opponent is warded off past the body...
2   ...and then he is turned around further with a low kick.
3   The action is continued by delivering two hooks to the kidneys.
5   Changing over to control the head and bending him over backwards.
6   Conclusion: Kick with the left knee to the kidneys.

3.12 Kidney region/Skin folds

Attack: Grab the skin folds in the kidney region with both hands and squeeze.

Effects: Pain (individually different).

Comments on use:
Like all nerve points, the degree of sensitivity and effectiveness is individually different – a harmless technique.

3.13 Ribs

See also the illustration in the Section on the "Breastbone."

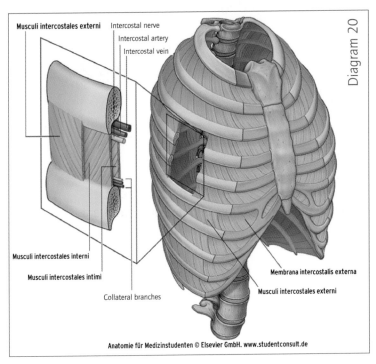

Musculi intercostales externi   Intercostal nerve
Intercostal artery
Intercostal vein

Diagram 20

Musculi intercostales interni

Musculi intercostales intimi

Collateral branches

Membrana intercostalis externa

Musculi intercostales externi

Anatomie für Medizinstudenten © Elsevier GmbH. www.studentconsult.de

The human has 12 pairs of ribs. The upper seven ribs are called sternal ribs (also called "true ribs") and these are directly connected to the breastbone (sternum) through the costal cartilage. Ribs 8-10 are called asternal ribs set at the cartilaginous ribcage, and the two lower ribs end freely in the chest muscles. Rib pairs 8-12 are defined as "false ribs." Ribs 11 and 12 are called "floating ribs" and end freely in the abdominal wall.

Attack: Strike, kick (foot, knee), body scissors – particularly aimed at the floating ribs.

1   The hook punch is blocked.
2   Controlling the neck.
3   Low kick at the short ribs using the shinbone.

Effects: Severe pain, breathing problems, bruises, breakage, internal injuries (liver, spleen, lungs, kidneys).

Due to the external effect, the function of the intercostal muscles can be affected (they raise and lower the ribs), and this hampers breathing. This may also affect the function of the diaphragm.

Generally, ribs heal well. Concerning fractures of the ribs, sometimes a pneumothorax condition occurs (air collecting in the pleural space). This affects the expansion of one or both lungs, which can be life-threatening depending on the severity. Also pulmonary contusion (can be fatal if untreated) or internal bleeding of the lungs (hematothorax) into the chest can occur. If a lung completely collapses, heart problems can result. This is because the heart is kept in place by the lungs, and in the case of a lung collapse, this function is absent. Injury to the spleen can occur when a left rib pierces it or it is ruptured independently. In fractures of the right-sided ribcage, damage to the liver can occur.

Comments on use:
Possible difficulty when faced by thick-muscled or corpulent persons, as well as anyone wearing thick-clothing.

1   The knee is lifted up to one side....
2   ....and brought onto the target with a whip-like hip movement.

3.14 Clavicle/Collarbone

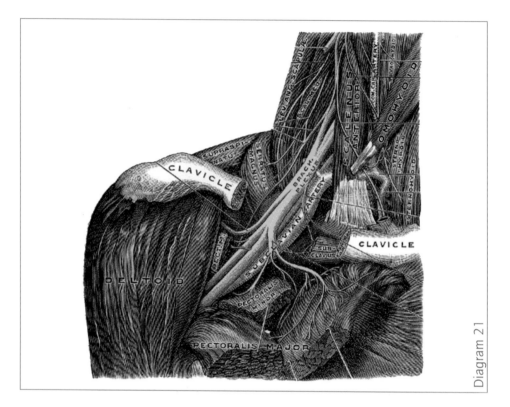

Human collarbone – view from above (here the right shoulder is shown)

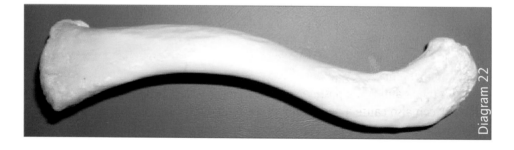

The collarbone is an S-shaped bone and is about 12-15 cms long. The collarbone is part of the shoulder girdle. It connects the breastbone with the acromion – part of the shoulder blade.

Attack: Strike (edge of the hand, base of the fist, elbow) in the cavity of the collarbone (the curving ridge nearest the shoulder).

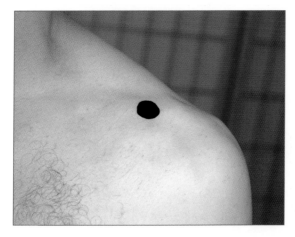

Target mark.

Effects: In adults, fracture of the collarbone is the second most common fracture after those of the radius. It is can be caused by a direct and (sometimes soft) blow to the collarbone. Complications include vascular damage (arteria subclavia) or nerve damage (plexus brachialis) where a large bruising is visible.

Brachialgia is the medical term for pain in the arm and is caused by mechanical rubbing or compression of the plexus brachialis. Where partial tearing (or other damage) of individual nerve fibers occur, this leads to partial immobility of the arm and the hand. The first indication of a problem is often a tingling feeling.

Where lesions of the plexus brachialis occur, complete impairment (paralysis) and sensitivity of the muscles of the upper extremities can appear.

Symptoms of a broken collarbone: Appearance of visible and palpable swelling or steps in the run of the bone, severe pain from pressure or when moved. The injured person brings his upper arm into a posture of relief and the shoulder protrudes clearly forward. The break can also cause a perforation of the lungs.

Comments on use:
The arm is rendered immobile and unusable.

Possible difficulty when faced by thick-muscled or corpulent persons, as well as anyone wearing thick-clothing.

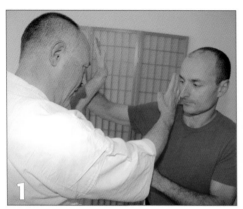 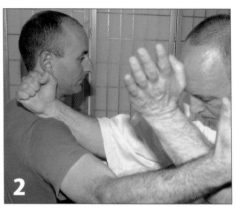

1   Strike with the edge of the hand at the collarbone (Shuto-Sakotsu-Uchi).

2   Strike using the forearm.

3.15   Solar plexus/Plexus coeliacus

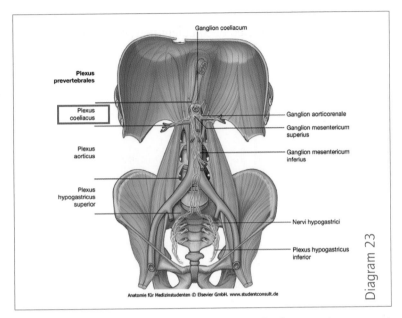

The solar plexus (plexus coeliacus) is a network of vegetative nerves, having its origin in front of the upper abdominal aorta (and thus lying relatively well away from the surface of the stomach). It runs to the stomach and the upper digestive organs. It is located between the 12th thoracic and the first lumbar vertebra.

It is supplied by the sympathetic (thoracic sympathikus) and parasympathetic (nervus vagus) parts of the vegetative nervous system.

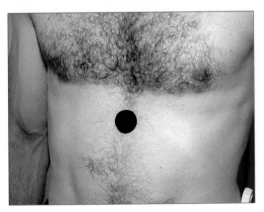

Attack: Hard punch/kick at a hand-sized area lying a little to the left of the center in the upper third of the line between the navel and the breastbone. The compression wave then reaches the plexus.

Target mark.

Effects:

1) The function of the plexus coeliacus is to stimulate the glands of the mucous membranes of the stomach and the upper digestive organs, as well as stimulation of the stomach muscles and the upper sections of the small intestine. However, it is also a control center: Harmful foreign particles entering the stomach, such as rotten or poisonous food, are immediately expelled – nausea and vomiting follow. Thus, the direction of the "peristaltic wave" is reversed and as a protective measure the contents of the stomach are brought up and expelled. In a reflex action, the stomach muscles are tensed in order to reach sufficient pressure to push past the valve in the esophagus.

Heavy mechanical strain leads to the same effect, especially when it happens during inhalation because at that moment the protective stomach muscles are relaxed and an external blow, such as a leg or punching technique, can have a full effect in depth.

2) A hit on the plexus coeliacus can also lead to unconsciousness:

An external blow can also cause a vagovasal syncope through the connection of the nervus vagus with the center for the heart rate and the heart. With a sudden, massive stimulation of the vegetative nervous system, the heart rate center in the hypothalamus overreacts and this suddenly opens the blood vessels of the intestine, the portal vein area, the liver, the kidneys and several other organs. There is a loss of blood pressure together with a short lack of blood circulation in the brain (a "blackout"), and the person collapses. Normally, this passes after a few seconds and one wakes up quickly because while lying down the blood pressure rapidly stabilizes itself.

3) Pain, difficulty in breathing.

4) It should be remembered that many of the internal organs, particularly the liver, spleen and also the kidneys, have a good circulatory flow of blood. If organs such as these are hit hard, there is a danger of rupturing the liver, spleen, the neighboring stomach (see appropriate section), or pancreatic necrosis (tissue death of the pancreas) wherein hidden internal bleeding ensues. Such internal bleeding is malicious precisely because it is invisible. This process can develop over a period of several days.

It is also possible that although the vein does break, it will be damaged to such an extent that if it is put under strain again (e.g., in sport), a spontaneous break accompanied by severe bleeding will occur. The bleeding can be very serious and even lead to death.

Comments on use:

Possible difficulty when faced by thick-muscled or corpulent persons, as well as anyone who is wearing thick clothing. When the person is breathing in, the effect is increased because the protective stomach muscles are relaxed.

1   Gyaku-tsuki punch at the solar plexus.

A quick punch at the solar plexus serves to break the resistance to being thrown here.

3.16 Coccyx

See the illustration in section 2.2 ("Nape of the neck").

The human coccyx is the lowest point of the sacral bone that, in turn, is at the end of the spine. The end of the spinal cord is not at the bottom of the spine (i.e., coccyx) but lies at the beginning of the lumbar part of the spine. Running downward in the direction of the coccyx are nerves (plexus coccygeus), which merely have a sensory (skin) function.

If kicked or one falls onto the coccyx, it can be dislocated, which is very painful. The injured person can hardly bear to sit because of the pain, and the healing process is long. Treatment by a physician is carried out rectally. An operation may also be necessary.

Attack: Kick with the knee (standing or lying down), kick.

1   The punch is warded off.
2   The opponent's head is turned and pinned to one's shoulder.
3   Knee kick at the coccyx.

Effects: Pain, minor sensory disturbance.

Comments on use:

In a standing position, one must be behind the other person.

1   Bringing back the kicking leg.
2   The knee kick is on its way.
3   On target!

157

3.17 Lower abdomen (Bladder, Intestines, Pubic bone)

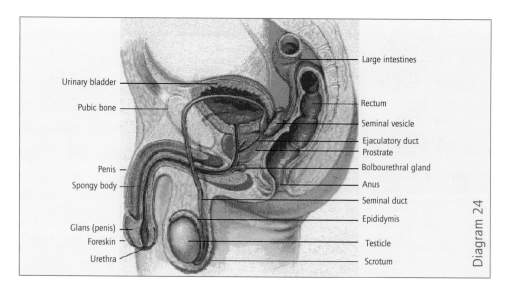

Diagram 24

See the illustration for "Intestines" and the section on the "Liver."

Attack: Punch, kick, knee kick.

1   Defensive gesture just before an incoming attack.
2   Preparing to kick.

3   Forward kick at the lower abdomen using the heel.

Effects: Pain from impact on abdomen, internal injuries, violent bowel movement.

The urinary bladder is pushed into the abdominal cavity only when the bladder is not quite so full. When the bladder is full and suffers an external traumatic blow, it can rupture and empty its contents into the abdominal cavity (intraperitoneal rupture of the bladder). Symptoms are pain in the lower abdomen and a strong urge to urinate while simultaneously being unable to do so. A particular danger is that of peritonitis.

Rupture of the intestinal wall is only possible following a blow hitting a large surface area (e.g., traffic accident). An injury in the region of the pubic symphysis (cartilage and ligament injuries) is possible.

Comments on use:
Thick-muscled or corpulent persons are vulnerable to attacks on the pubic symphysis.

4 Attack points on the arms

4.1 Skin of the arm

Skin in the area behind the upper arm.

Attack: Pinching.

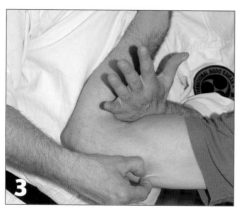

1 Grab the lapel.
2 Pick up the thin fold of skin.
3 The opponent's elbow is pinned to one's own body.

Effects: Pain – In the corium (deep inner layer of skin), there are free nerve endings (pain receptors). The thickness varies with the area of the body (up to 200 per sq cm of skin).

Comments on use:
Again, here the degree of pain and the effectiveness differ between persons; can be used as a freeing technique.

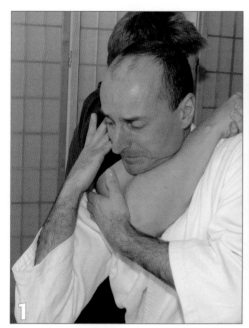 

1   With an attack using a Hadaka-jime (strangulation with the bare arms), the larynx is protected in the bend of the opponent's elbow. The skin at the rear of the upper arm is pinched hard, quickly and repeatedly. This causes overstimulation of the area that can be added to by biting into the biceps.

4.2   Biceps/Musculus biceps brachii

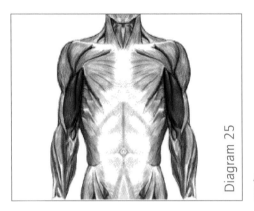

Diagram 25

Attack: Punch with the fist, side of the hand, elbow.

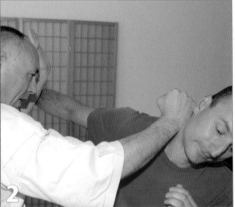

1   The swinging punch is blocked and, at the same time, countered by a strike at the biceps.
2   After the shock tactic on the biceps, the counterattack is continued directly using a hammer fist or strike with the ulna at the neck.

Effects: When delivered with sufficient force, a blow on the biceps is extremely painful and results in temporary loss of the mobility in the arm.

Damage to organs or parts of the body, caused by external direct, blunt force without visible injury to the skin is known as bruising. This creates an edema (swelling) of the tissues and extravasation of blood from the damaged capillaries in the surrounding tissue, which can appear as a bruise. Generally, pain is immediate and limits mobility. In cases of larger swellings, stiffening of the muscle can occur.

Similar events occur in contusions, which is when the body tissue is pressed together.

In a torn muscle fiber, the reticular fibers are damaged and local inflammatory symptoms occur. At the same time, local reduction of tonus (state of tension in the muscles) is apparent in the damaged area. With tears in larger muscles, sometimes clear recesses or knotting of the muscles in the affected area can be seen.

The biceps are innervated by the nervus musculocutaneus.

Thrombosis is unlikely.

Comments on use:
The strike must be well aimed and directed at the bones of the upper arm.

 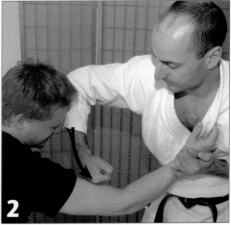

In this sequence, the punch is not made flat so that the knuckles can bore into the muscle.

4.3 Elbows

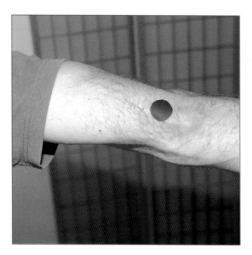

The elbow joint joins the bone of the upper arm (humerus) with the two bones of the lower arm – the radius and the ulna.

Attack: Strike against the outstretched elbow joint.

NOTE: When attacking the target, the elbow joint is not the tip of the elbow, but rather the hollow proximal, inward to the body from the tip of the elbow.

Effects: Joint dislocation, or luxation (Latin: luxatio), occurs when bones in a joint become displaced or misaligned. A luxation causes serious injury to the joint. The bones comprising a joint cannot carry out their function without causing extreme damage to the joint capsule. It is often combined with a fracture. When forcefully stretched out, the olecranon (tip of the elbow joint nearest the body) at the end of the ulna can break.

In such cases, damage to the nervus ulnaris ("funny bone") and the nervus radialis can occur with subsequent paralysis of the arm and/or hand. Additionally, the upper arm artery (arteria brachialis) can be damaged.

Comments on use:
Here, one notes that the transition between Kyusho and lever techniques has no clear dividing line. Well-trained muscles provide certain protection against the required overstretching.

1 The fist attack is warded off....

2 ....with a Wing-Tsun like movement (Bong-Sao).

3 The wrist is grabbed.

4 Stretch using an arm lever.

5 Bring up the arm in preparation to deliver a strike with the ulna.

6 Strike. **CAREFUL!** Damage to the elbow joint.

7 Bring opponent to the ground.

4.4 Hand

For an illustration, see the section on the "Wrist."

The hand is innervated by three nerves: nervus ulnaris, nervus medianus, and nervus radialis. The wrist joint is connected to the metacarpus, which consists of the five long metacarpal bones.

Attack: Press the tip of the thumb into the hollow between metacarpal bones 2 and 3 or 3 and 4 in the triangle between the thumb and the forefinger; strike the metacarpal area with the knuckles.

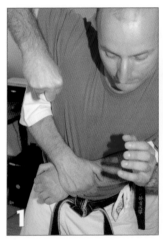  

1   Reaction to the clinch: Strike using the knuckles of the fist (Nadaka-Ken) at the back of the hand. This frees one from the clinch attack and opens the possibility for follow-up techniques.

Effects: Nerve and skin pain (skin over bone surfaces) or fractures.

Comments on use:
Like all nerve points, the degree of sensitivity, as well as effect achieved, is individually different. Mostly used as a freeing technique.

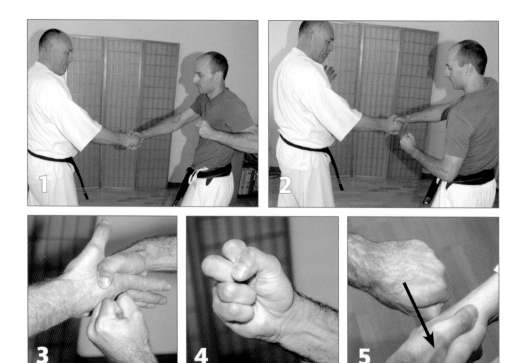

1   Attempt to squeeze the hand.
2   The defender retreats to one side away from the opponent.
4   How to hold the hand.
5   Using a strike with the joint of the thumb is also possible.

1   With a little practice, it is also possible to combine the defense of a strike at the back of the hand with a hand sweeping movement.

4.5 Wrist

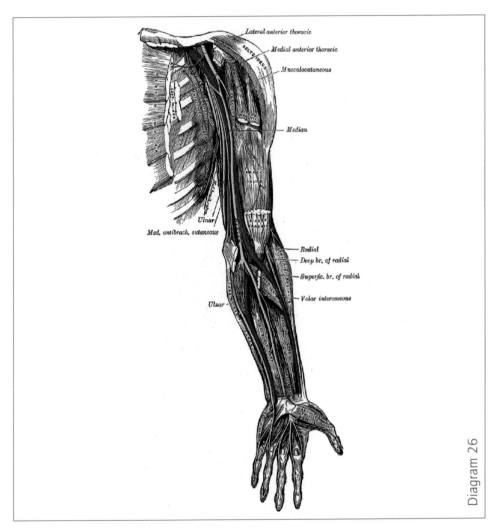

Lateral anterior thoracic
Medial anterior thoracic
Musculocutaneous
Median
Ulnar
Med. antibrach, cutaneous
Radial
Deep br. of radial
Superfic. br. of radial
Volar interosseous
Ulnar

Diagram 26

The nervus medianus runs from the armpit over the inside of the upper arm and then enters the forearm on the side of the palm of the hand. The nerve lies relatively superficially above the hand.

Attack: Pressure using the tip of the thumb between the tendons on the inside of the wrist. Strike using the base of the fist or knuckles.

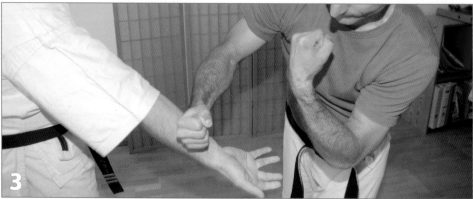

1 Attack: Grab wrist.

2 Counter: Strike in the direction of the face in order to obstruct attacker and to stretch his arm.

3 Free self from the grip by striking just above the wrist.

Effects: Nerve pain (neuralgia) can be felt after pressure applied (compare the statements in the Introduction). Additionally, the impact has an effect on other structures (tendons, blood vessels).

Comments on use:
Like all nerve points, the degree of sensitivity, as well as effect achieved, is individually different. Mostly used as a freeing technique.

1   The grip is countered by using a shock technique.
2   The freeing action is begun by delivering a strike at the wrist.
3   Stretch the opponent's arm while executing an obstructing action at his face.
4   Pull up the arm to strike.
5   By striking at the wrist, the opponent is turned so that his back is toward the defender.
6   Option: Use the elbow to strike downward at the wrist.

4.6   The nails

Attack: Scratch with your own nails.

Effects: Very painful scratch wounds.

Comments on use: Use as a freeing technique; very effective.

A good example – it's about efficiency, not preciseness nor elegance.

4.7 Median nerve/Nervus medianus

For description, see section on the "Wrist."

Attack: Pincer grip with the thumb pressing at the start of the biceps tendon against the nervus medianus.

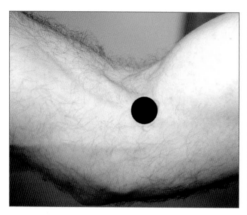

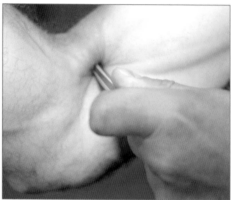

Target mark.   Direction of pressure

Effects: Nerve pain (neuralgia) can be felt after pressure applied (see the statements in the Introduction).

Comments on use:
Like all nerve points, the degree of sensitivity, as well as effect achieved, is individually different. Well-trained muscles and clothing also provide protection.

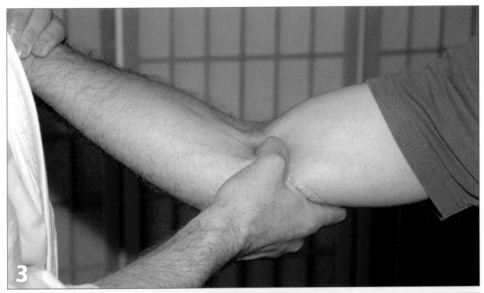

1 The grip on the lapel is countered directly by striking toward the face with the ball of the hand.

2 The attacking arm is brought under control and the pressure on the median nerve is applied.

3 Close-up.

4 The opponent is brought off balance using a Kanetsu-Geri kick (side-kick against the opponent's knee).

4.8   Radial nerve/Nervus radialis

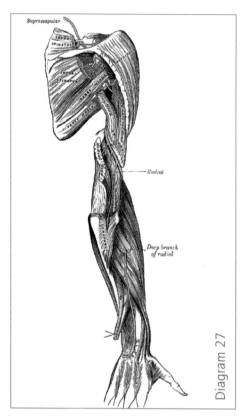

Diagram 27

View from rear.

The nervus radialis (radial nerve) is a nerve of the plexus brachialis group. It innervates the extensor muscles of the elbow joint, wrist joint, and finger joints, as well as the area of skin on the rear side of the upper arm, the underside of the lower arm, and the back of the hand.

It runs down the middle of the upper arm between the heads of the triceps (musculus triceps brachii), twists around, lies directly over the bone of the upper arm, and then moves outward over the elbow. It emerges through the supinator muscle – the muscle responsible for the outward twisting movement of the hand and lower arm.

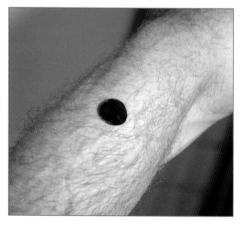

Attack:
Upper arm: Punch or pressure with the shinbone.

Lower arm: Strike (ulna, hammer fist punch) or applying pressure with the thumb (pincer grip) in the upper third or pincer grip of the brachioradial muscle (see the illustration for the "Wrist") just below the crook of the arm.

Target mark.

Effects: Nerve pain (neuralgia) can be felt after pressure applied (compare the statements in the Introduction).

When the nervus radialis is affected, the wrist and finger extensors can be paralyzed, and the fingers and wrist are bent backwards. If the damage is further up, there can also be a paralysis of the triceps, and the elbow joint cannot be stretched out straight. Simultaneously, there will be a loss of sensitivity in the area.

Comments on use:

Like all nerve points, the degree of sensitivity, as well as effect achieved, is individually different. Finding the right spot (especially when applying pressure) requires a lot of practice.

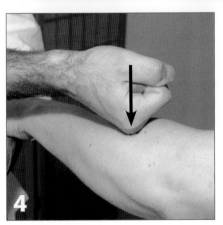

1	The attack is warded off using the back of the hand.
2	After grabbing the wrist, the arm is pulled back for a counter strike.
3	Strike with the edge of the hand onto the radial nerve.
4	As an alternative, the strike can be made with the knuckles of the fist.

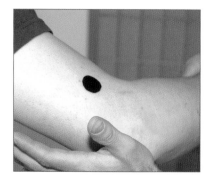

Target mark.

The radial nerve is located in the area of the upper arm. To find it, place a cupped hand around the tip of the training partner's elbow. Stretch with the thumb onto the skin, and you have found it.

Generally speaking, one has to exert a great deal of pressure here, which is quite possible when on the ground. Here, the shinbone is sawn across the nerve – backwards and forward.

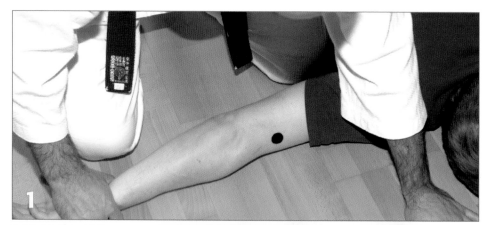

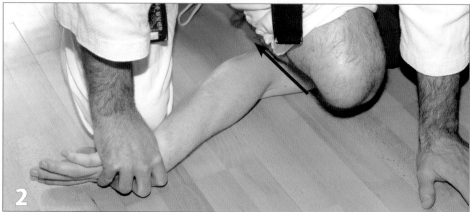

Counter to being grabbed by the lapel: Hook punch with the knuckles of the fist onto the radial nerve.

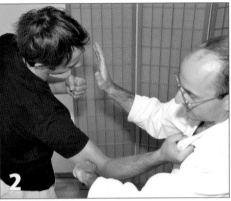

Rotate the opponent's elbow inward. By continuing the rotation, the attacker is brought to the ground.

A similar strike can be used to start a throw. Throw backwards like O-Soto-Gari.

4.9　Ulnar nerve/Nervus ulnaris

This is the nerve known as the "funny bone." If the nerve is affected, one can feel the effect right up into the little finger.

For an illustration, see the section on the "Wrist" (Page 169).

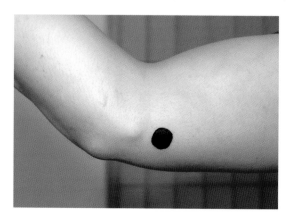

Attack: Strike with the knuckles.

Target mark on upper arm region.

Example of use:

 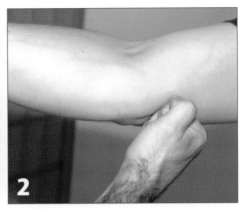

Effects: When hit, there is a severe pain (neuralgia) felt right up to the tips of the little and ring fingers (see statements in Introduction).

Comments on use: The target area on the upper arm is very small so the angle of the strike must be precise. Otherwise, it is a good example of a Kyusho vulnerable point on the nerves. The target on the lower arm can be easily struck, particularly, just as he adopts an on-guard position.

1   Target spot on the region of the lower arm.
2   Right uppercut at the ulnar nerve on the lower arm.

4.10 Inside of the upper arm

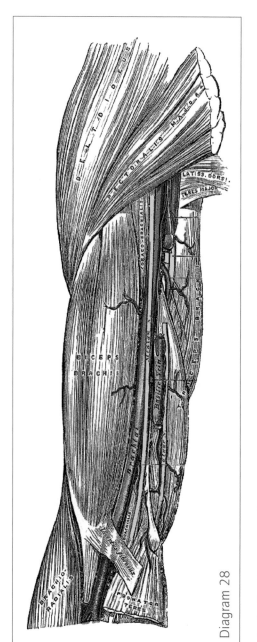

Diagram 28

The basilic vein (shown in blue in the diagram) and the upper arm artery (arteria brachialis – shown in red in the diagram) run down the groove between the extensor and the flexor muscle structure on the inside of the upper arm (sulcus bicipitalis). This artery is a continuation of the axillary artery, and it supplies the whole arm with blood. It is accompanied by nerves (shown in yellow in the diagram) running alongside, which belong to the plexus brachialis (nervus medianus and nervus ulnaris, nervus cutaneus antebrachii medialis, and nervus cutaneus brachii medialis).

Attack: Punch.

Effects: Nerve pain (neuralgia) can be felt after pressure is applied (see the statements in the Introduction).

Unlikely scenarios:

Possibility of a venous thrombosis caused by a massive blow, the result of which can be pulmonary embolism and, in certain circumstances, heart attack.

In cases of an arterial thrombosis, there is a danger of damage to the coronary vessels (heart infarction), the vessels supplying the brain (stroke), and the leg arteries. The cause of arterial thrombosis is damage or scarring of the vascular wall.

The extremity affected is usually cold and pale, the pulse can no longer be felt, and severe pain starts. The function is extremely limited.

Comments on use:
Like all nerve points, the degree of sensitivity, as well as effect achieved, is individually different. Well-trained muscles and thick clothing add protection.

In order to increase target precision, it will be advantageous to make contact with the outside of the upper arm with the other hand. The strike should be aimed at the bone of the upper arm.

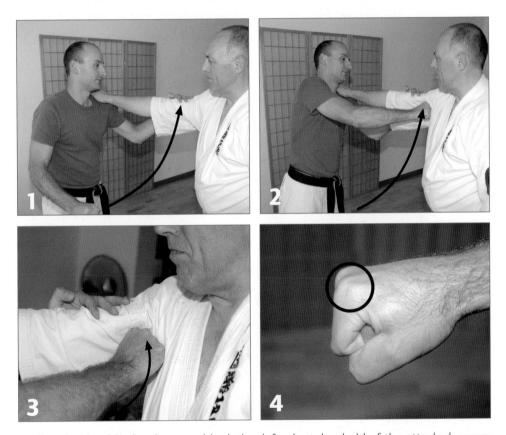

1 After the shoulder has been grabbed, the defender takes hold of the attacker's upper arm firmly on the outside. **2** Short punch with the inside of the fist at the inside of the attacker's upper arm. Principle: Make a kind of sandwich. **3** Close-up. **4** Target area.

1 If the opponent holds the arm diagonally, the arm has to be rotated before delivering the punch.

4.11 Triceps - Final chord

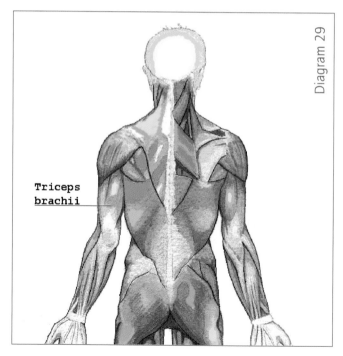

Diagram 29

Triceps
brachii

The triceps is sometimes called a three-headed muscle because there are three bundles of muscles joining together at the elbow as a common final chord in the lower third of the upper arm.

Attack: Apply pressure using the shinbone or base joint of the forefinger.

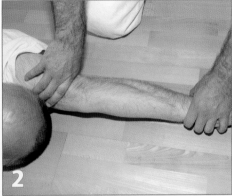
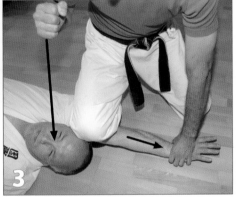

1   The outstretched arm is pinned to the floor.

2   Close-up.

3   Pinned down using the shinbone. This is very painful because the whole of the body weight is pushing down on the arm. It is possible to conclude the sequence by using a hammer fist punch to the face.

Effects: Pain from pressure on the tendon, which can also involve the ulnar nerve (runs directly over the "funny bone" next to the elbow hinge joint with the bone of the upper arm − see the section the "Wrist"). Damage to these areas is indicated by numbness in the little finger, on the outside part of the ring finger, and on the ball of the little finger.

Comments on use:
Like all nerve points, the degree of sensitivity and effectiveness is individually different.

5 Attack Points on the Legs

5.1 Achilles tendon

1 Prepare to kick.
2 Execute a Yoko-Geri (side-kick) at the Achilles tendon.
3 Close-up.

Attack: Stamping kick, using the shinbone to apply pressure.

Effects: Tear, pain; when foot is balanced on toes, also ankle and foot injury.

Comments on use:
Just as with the nerve points, the degree of sensitivity and effectiveness is individually different.

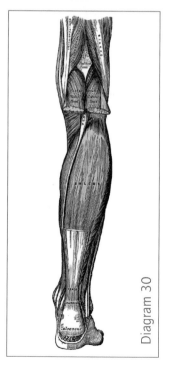

Diagram 30

1   Defensive low kick using the shinbone.
3   Grab the diagonal shoulder.
4   Inside sweep.

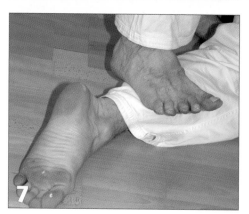

5   The opponent's balance is broken.
6   Concluding technique: Stamping on the Achilles heel with the foot on tiptoe...
7   ...or with the foot lying flat.

5.2   Instep

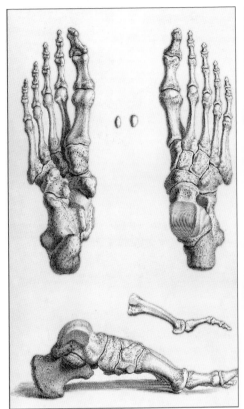

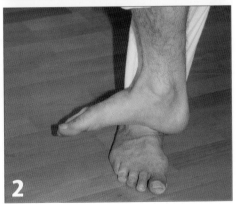

1   Clinch from behind. The leg is lifted up and rotated outward. The edge of the foot is brought down from the opponent's shinbone below the knee onto the foot.

2   The strike uses the shape of the shinbone to run down the leg onto the foot.

Attack: Stamping kick.

Effects: Breakage of the instep bones.

Comments on use:
For once, high heels would be an advantage in combat.

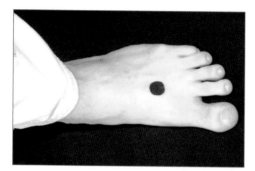

Target mark.

1   The nerves between the toes of the instep (medial plantar nerves) can also be targeted for various actions. Here, the opponent's foot is pinned down with pressure from the defender's big toe in the hollow between the big toe and the remainder of the instep – painful!

5.3   Skin on the inside of the thigh

Attack: Pinching.

 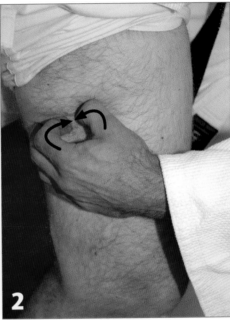

1   Headlock attack is freed by pinching the inside of the thigh firmly.
2   Close-up.

Effects: Pain; free nerve endings (pain receptors) can be found in the dermis. Their distribution varies according to the body area (up to 200 per sq cm of skin).

Comments on use:
Like all nerve points, the degree of sensitivity, as well as effect achieved, is individually different. Thick clothing adds protection. This can be used as a freeing technique.

5.4   Knee

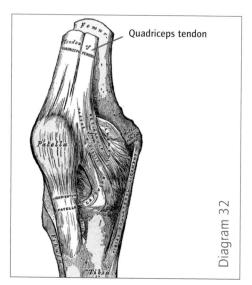

Quadriceps tendon

Diagram 32

Right knee viewed from front.

Attack: Kick (Yoko-Geri. Kakato-Geri, driving Mae-Geri kick at the kneecap.

2   In a direct attack at the kneecap, there is a danger of the kick slipping away because of the small size of the target.

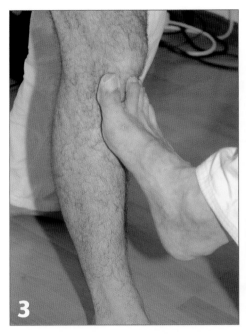

4   By turning the foot outward (Teisoku-Geri, the sole of the foot) the target area on the opponent is made larger, which increases the precision of the kick.

Effects: Immobility, pain, shock.

The knee joint is the connection between the upper and lower leg. It is formed by the lower end of the femur, the upper end of the tibia, the patella, the collateral and cruciate ligaments, and the two menisci.

The knee joint is stabilized by a pair of cruciate ligaments running downward on the side of the joint.

The cruciate ligaments (front and back) stabilize the knee and prevent the articulating surfaces from slipping forward or backwards and inhibiting the rotation. The classic injury of the anterior cruciate ligament occurs when the knee is flexed and violent internal rotation occurs.

Damage to the meniscus occurs mainly when there is an intensive and rapid twist of the knee joint.

Following luxation (occurs when bones in a joint become displaced or misaligned), the knee will likely be unable to be used properly. A luxation causes serious injury to the joint. The bones comprising a joint cannot carry out their function without causing extreme damage to the joint capsule. Damage to the patella generally leaves no long-term problems and heals well when treated properly.

A kick in the hollow behind the knee can, in addition to injury to the blood vessels and the nerves in this area (especially when shoes are worn), cause a transverse fracture of the kneecap due to muscle tension. A transverse fracture of the kneecap must always be operated upon, otherwise the great strength of the quadriceps will lead to further medical complications.

When there is luxation of the patella, usually blood vessels are damaged and a bruise appears. Speedy reconstruction is important to reduce damage to the cartilage.

Isolated ruptures of the anterior cruciate ligament are rare. Often there are simultaneous injuries of the collateral ligament on the side and/or menisci. One speaks of a combination of injuries. ("Unhappy triad": cruciate ligament, collateral ligament and meniscus.)

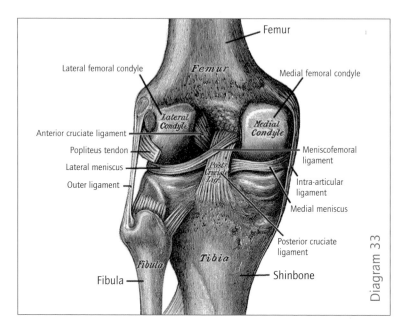

Diagram 33

Left knee joint
(from rear)

A lateral kick can lead (at best) to a painful pulled ligament coupled with restricted movement (because it is painful). If the knee is overstretched, an injury to the meniscus can occur when excessive force is involved. Additionally, there can be injuries to the collateral ligaments.

Comments on use:
Easily targeted; well-trained muscles offer a certain amount of protection.

5.5 Hollow of the knee

The tibial nerve is a continuation of the nervus ischiadicus (see its section), which runs through the "popliteal fossa;" for an illustration, see the section on the "Achilles tendon."

Attack: Kick, pressing the thumb into the hollow of the knee or popliteal fossa.

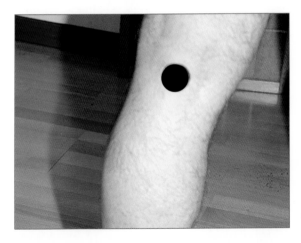

Target mark.

Effects: Nerve pain (neuralgia) can be felt after pressure is applied (see the statements in the Introduction).

Comments on use:
Like all nerve points, the degree of sensitivity, as well as effect achieved, is individually different. Thick clothing adds protection. Its use is limited.

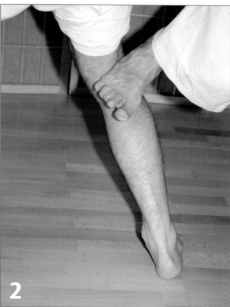

1   Executing a Kanetsu-Geri at the hollow of the knee.
2   Close-up.

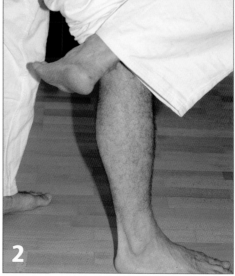

1   Low kick behind the knee.

1   Defense against a headlock: Press the thumb into the hollow of the knee.

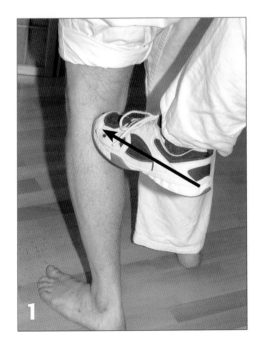

1   Shoes can also be used to deliver a kick at the politeal fossa.

5.6   Sciatic nerve/Nervus ischiadicus

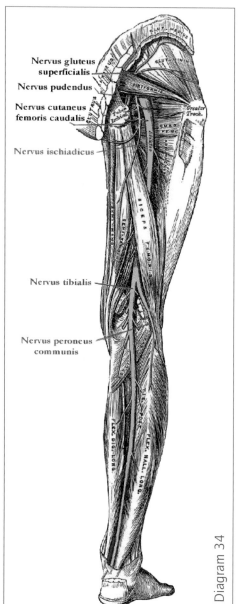

Nervus gluteus
superficialis

Nervus pudendus

Nervus cutaneus
femoris caudalis

Nervus ischiadicus

Nervus tibialis

Nervus peroneus
communis

Diagram 34

The sciatic nerve runs on the extensor side of the hip joint, and then down at the back of the thigh. It is covered by the knee flexors, and then continues behind the knee where it goes through the "popliteal fossa." It is divided into the tibial nerve and the common peroneal nerve (common fibular nerve). On its way, it branches out providing the motor innervation of some of the thigh muscles.

Attack: Kick (shin, knee), best with relaxed muscles.

Effects: Paralysis of the sciatic nerve due to pressure, strain or deformation (for example by sitting on uneven surfaces or by sitting on the wallet in the back pocket), or by incorrect practice when intragluteal injections are given, causes the failure of tendons and outer rotator muscles in the thigh. Neuralgia (see the Introduction) in the sciatic nerve occurs when the nerve is stretched (strained knee, inflected hip) as a characteristic pain in the lower back and buttocks. In addition, a numbness, muscular weakness and other difficulties can be experienced when moving the leg. Typically, these symptoms only appear on one side of the body.

1 A Mae-Geri kick is warded off.
2 Subsequent low kick at the back of the thigh.
3 Knee kick at the sciatic nerve (causing a bruise on the thigh).
4 The opponent is brought to the floor.

Comments on use:
Like all nerve points, the degree of sensitivity, as well as effect achieved, is individually different. It can be used as a freeing technique. Easily targeted.

5.7   Outer side of the thigh

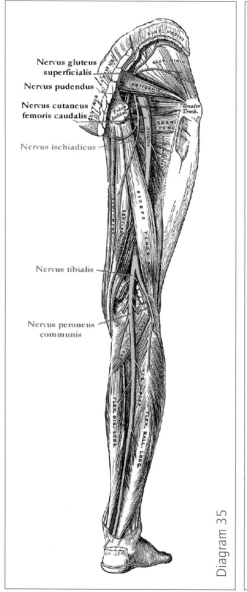

Nervus gluteus
superficialis

Nervus pudendus

Nervus cutaneus
femoris caudalis

Nervus ischiadicus

Nervus tibialis

Nervus peroneus
communis

Diagram 35

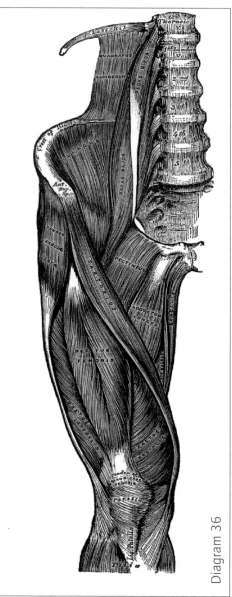

Diagram 36

See also the illustration in the section of the "Inner side of the thigh."

Attack: Kick (shin, knee).

1   Start a low kick.
2   Execute.
3   The leg is "kicked through," so to speak. The kick is followed up and performed as if one were kicking at the opponent's leg "through the air."

Effects:

Muscles: The muscles that are affected are the musculus vastus lateralis (on the outer side of the thigh) – one of the front muscles of the thigh – or the musculus tensor fasciae latae (Latin: tensor of the fascia of the thigh); the latter has the shape of a flat rectangle. The tendon is a strip-like reinforcement of the fascia latae and extends over the entire length of the thigh. This reinforcement is called also the iliotibial band.

Damage to organs or parts of the body caused by external direct, blunt force without visible injury to the skin is known as bruising. This creates an edema (swelling) of the tissues and extravasation of blood from the damaged capillaries in the surrounding tissue, which can appear as a bruise. Generally, pain is immediate and limits mobility. In cases of larger swellings, stiffening of the muscle can occur.

Similar events occur in contusions, which is when the body tissue is pressed together.

In a torn muscle fiber, the reticular fibers are damaged and local inflammatory symptoms occur. At the same time, local reduction of tonus (state of tension in the muscles) is apparent in the damaged area. With tears in larger muscles, sometimes clear recesses or knotting of the muscles in the affected area can be seen.

Thrombosis is unlikely.

Tears of the fascia skin are hardly likely; however, compartment syndrome may be possible (swelling in the muscle with reduced blood circulation, increase of pressure and, if not treated, possible necrosis).

Nerves: Injury to these is unlikely.

Affected nerves can include the femoral nerve (has an effect on the vastus lateralis muscle), the nervus gluteus superior (the "upper gluteal nerve" has an effect on the musculus tensor fasciae latae), as well as the fibularis communis/ peronaeus communis nerves (easily felt in the area of the knee joint) from the hollow in the back of the knee downward in the lower thigh. In both cases, the consequences are pain, "paralysis" of the leg and therefore instability.

1   Block the backhanded strike.
2   Pin the opponent's shoulders.

3   Knee kick with the thigh (bruise!).

Comments on use:
Like all nerve points, the degree of sensitivity, as well as effect achieved, is individually different. Well-trained muscles offer good protection. Easily targeted.

5.8   Inner side of the thigh

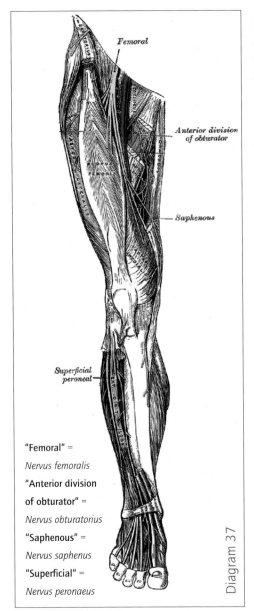

"Femoral" =

Nervus femoralis

"Anterior division

of obturator" =

Nervus obturatorius

"Saphenous" =

Nervus saphenus

"Superficial" =

Nervus peronaeus

Diagram 37

In the thigh, the nervus saphenus (saphenous nerve) branches off from the nervus femoralis (femoral nerve). It lies along in front (along the inside) of the thigh artery and emerges at the surface here.

In addition, in the upper third of the thigh, one finds the nervus obturatorious that innervates the adductors of the leg.

Attack: Kick using the shinbone or knee, inside edge of the hand.

Effects:
Muscles: Damage to organs or parts of the body caused by external direct, blunt force without visible injury to the skin is known as bruising. This creates an edema (swelling) of the tissues and extravasation of blood from the damaged capillaries in the surrounding tissue and can appear as a bruise. Generally, pain is immediate and limits mobility. In cases of larger swellings, stiffening of the muscle can occur.

Similar events occur in contusions, which is when the body tissue is pressed together.

In a torn muscle fiber, the reticular fibers are damaged and local inflammatory symptoms occur. At the same time, local reduction of tonus (state of tension in the muscles) is apparent in the damaged area. With tears in larger muscles, sometimes clear recesses or knotting of the muscles in the affected area can be seen.

It is also possible that compartment syndrome may develop (swelling in the muscle with reduced blood circulation, increase of pressure and, if not treated, possible necrosis).

Thrombosis is likely because the vena saphena (saphenous vein) can be so affected that clots of blood can find their way into the lung arteries and cause a lung embolism. Consequences include a drop in blood pressure, damage to the lungs, and collapse of the circulatory system, which is fatal.[14]

Nerves:
Due to the numerous muscles, which are innervated by the femoral nerve, severe movement disorders or loss of stability can occur; possibly inflammation (neuritis).

1   Headlock – head to head.
2   Attack at the inside of the thigh using a Haito-Uchi (inside edge of the hand). If the strike lands in the genitals instead of the inside of the thigh, there is a danger that the freeing technique has failed. The opposite happens as the attacker's reflex to the strike is to tighten his stranglehold.

Comments on use:
The degree of sensitivity, as well as effect achieved, is individually different. Not as easily targeted as the outside of the thigh.

1 The diagonal shoulder is controlled following the attack. (The defender's left hand pins the attacker's left shoulder following the attack.)

1 The attacker delivers a low kick.
2 The kick is cushioned, i.e., the force of the kick is dissipated by yielding the blocked leg.
3 Actively kicking back with the leg.

4 The opponent is forced to move his leg back.
5 Counterattack: Kinteki-Geri.
6 Alternative counterattack: Uchimomo-Geri (inside low kick at the thigh)

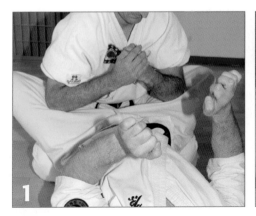 

1 + 2 Use in groundwork – freeing from a scissor grip.

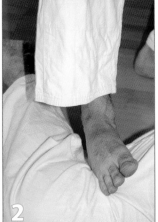

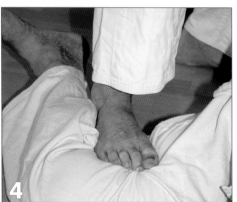

1 Additional use – pinning opponent down on the ground....

2 .....with the outside of the foot (Sokuto) or....

3 ..... with the toes or ball of the foot.

1 Wearing shoes can increase the effectiveness of its use.

5.9   Shinbone/Tibia

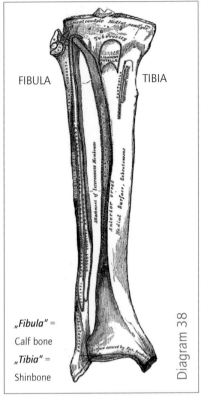

FIBULA   TIBIA

Diagram 38

„*Fibula*" =
Calf bone
„*Tibia*" =
Shinbone

Bones of the right lower leg – viewed from the front.

Attack: Kick, "sawing" with one's own shinbone.

1   From a clinch...
2   ....the opponent's shinbone is stamped down on – short and hard.
3   His leg is stretched out by this, giving space to deliver follow-up knee kicks or throws.

Effects:
Inflammation of the leg skin, break (thrombosis/embolism; pulmonary embolus, stroke).

On the face of the shaft, there is a strip of bone (crista anterior) that runs downward. This strip of bone is directly under the skin, forming the medial surface of the shaft.

The shin is surrounded by the periosteum membrane or bone skin and consists of a solid connective tissue layer that abuts the bone. The inner layer contains the nerves and blood vessels making the periosteum, in contrast to the bone itself, very sensitive to pain. When the shin is kicked, the vessels of the periosteum tear and a bruise between bone and periosteum appears. However, the sharp pain is felt for only a few minutes. By mechanical action, there may also be painful and long-lasting inflammation of the bone skin (periostitis).

Because the tibia runs just under the skin, open fractures are relatively common. There is a risk of thrombosis). In every injury of the lower limbs, there is a risk of a thrombosis (vascular blood clots). With large bone fractures, there is the risk of an embolism caused by a blockage of fat droplets. An embolism is a complete or partial obstruction in a blood vessel due to a blood clot or other foreign matter that gets stuck while traveling through the bloodstream.

Comments on use:
Good as an opening technique or as a possibility of taking the opponent off balance at short reach.

Example of "sawing" with one's own shin:

Sawing is itself not very pleasant for the defender. However, while the pressure he applies is spread over the whole of his shin, it is the same place on the attacker's tibia that is constantly being attacked.

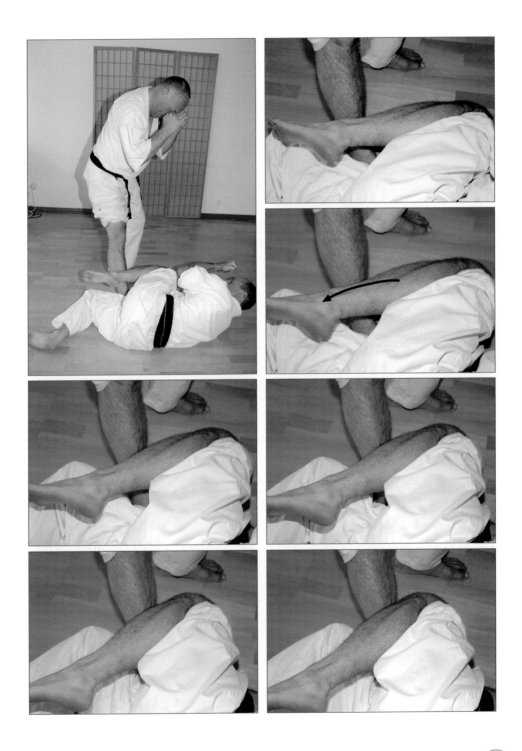

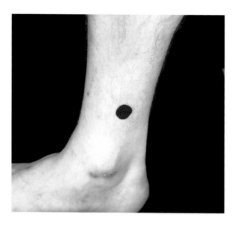

Target mark.

The most sensitive spot on the shinbone is the area at its side and rear just above the ankle.

In the **following sequence**, this is used to double the effect.

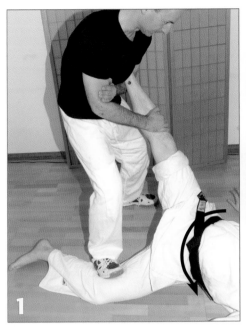

1   Even if the opponent turns on one side following the foot lever, the inside edge of the tibia can easily be used for control. Pressure is then created using the radius.

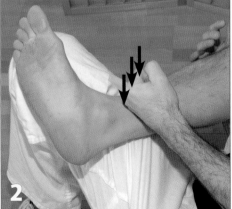

1   If the opponent is holding you from behind in a scissor grip, then the rear edge of the shinbone can be "worked on" firmly by repeatedly using the knuckles of the fist.

213

5.10   Calves

Compare with the illustration in the section on the "Outer side of the thigh."

Attack: Kick, pressure (edge of the foot, shinbone, thumb).

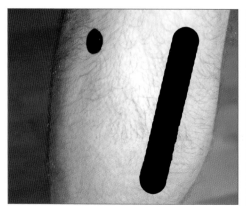

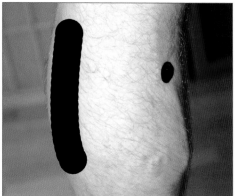

Target mark on left leg, rear side and inside of the calf

Target mark on right leg, rear side and inside of the calf

Effects: Pain caused by strike/pressure.
Rear side of the calf: Nervus tibialis, nervus suralis.
Inside of the calf: Branches of the nervus tibialis.
Outer side of the calf: Nervus peronaeus communis (= Nervus fibularis communis).

When pressure is applied, nerve pain can be felt (neuralgia) (see the statements in the Introduction). There is also a risk of thrombosis when a kick causes a traumatic injury.

Comments on use:
The degree of sensitivity, as well as effect achieved, is individually different, so a more precise approach is required to penetrate deeply when applying pressure; the strike at the heel does not require the same precision because of the larger impact achieved. Basically, it is sufficient that the calf just below the knee (inside/outer side/ rear side) is targeted, so that in addition to bringing the opponent off balance, there is also pain. In this way, the effectiveness of the leg throw is increased.

1 Clinch situation: Back kick with the heel at the outside edge of the calf.
2 The attacker tries to lift the defender up. The latter responds by lifting his heel to make a strike.

1 Scissor grip on the body from behind is freed by pressing the thumb into the inside of the calf.
2 Close-up.
3 Pain!

 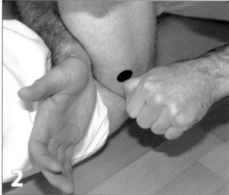

1   The bent knee lever that follows can be made more painful by applying additional pressure on outer side of the calf using the knuckle of the thumb.

5.11   Fibula

See the illustration in the section on the "Shinbone."

Attack: Kick using the shinbone/edge of the foot (opponent standing or in the kneeling position).

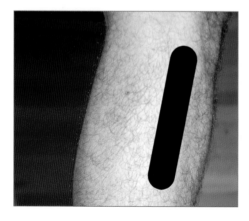

Target mark (right lower leg).

Effects: Break, not possible to put weight on the foot.

Comments on use:
Target is easily reached and effectiveness is also good.

1   The punch is warded off.   **2**   Grab round the elbow to control it.
4   In a rapid, semi-circular sweep, the inside of the shinbone just above the ankle is used to kick the opponent's fibula.

1   Technique used to pin the opponent to the floor.

1   The opponent's leg is pinned by the ankle.
2   Grab the hollow at the back of the opponent's knee and bend.
3   Using this action, the opponent's body is turned over.

4 Starting the twisting movement.

6 Pinning the leg onto the floor by placing your weight on the fibula with your shinbone.

6   Special Techniques

In this section, we illustrate two special techniques.

If the opponent has nothing on or is wearing little clothing, controlling him is still possible. Irrespective of how muscular the opponent is, or how little subcutaneous fatty tissue he has, the fleshy part of his skin can always be gathered up like grasping a cloth duster. **CAREFUL!** Very painful.

Gripping technique: The open hand is placed on the triceps and the fingers are pulled together in a gripping action. At a certain point, the skin can be gripped like picking up a fold in a cloth. The opponent can be controlled easily because of the pain.

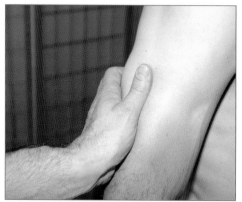 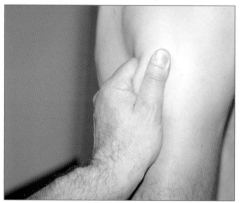

The fold of skin, held between the thumb and the forefinger, can be used for a follow-up attack at the neck.

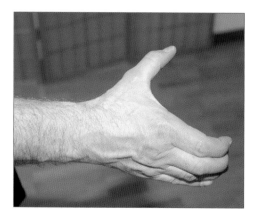

How to hold the hand.

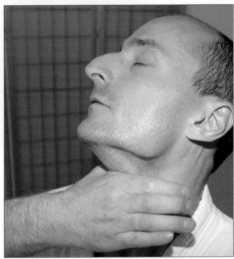

If the opponent is wearing very thick clothing, then many of the options we have shown will be ineffective.

In this case, the maxim is:

If you cannot ignore him or beat him, then make him your friend!

Appendix

Recommended literature

Adams, Brian. *Deadly Karate Blows – The Medical Implications.* California, 1998.

Christensen, Loren W. *Fighting the Pain Resistant Attacker.* USA, 2010.

Clark, Rick. *Pressure-point Fighting: A Guide to the Secret Heart of Asian Martial Arts.* USA, 2001.

Dillman, George A. *Kyusho Jitsu.* USA, 1993.

Dillman, George A. *Advanced Pressure Point Fighting.* USA, 1994.

Dr. Czerwenka-Wenkstetten, Heribert. *Kanon des Nippon JuJitsu.* Tyrolia-Verlag, 1993.

Drake Richard L; A. Wayne Vogl and Adam W. M. Mitchell. *Gray's Anatomy for Students.* Churchill Livingstone, 2004.

Goldacre, Ben. *Bad Science: Quacks, Hacks, and Big Pharma Flacks.* Fourth Estate, 2008

Höller, Jürgen & Maluschka, Axel & Reinisch, Stefan. *Selbstverteidigung für Frauen und Mädchen.* Aachen 2007.

Kawaishi, Mikinosuke. *My Method of Self-defense.* London, 1962.

Kelly, Michael. *Death Touch: The Science Behind the Legend of Dim-Mak.* USA, 2001.

Kim, Sang H. *Vital Point Strikes.* USA, 2008.

Morris, Vince. *The Secret Art of Pressure Point Fighting: Techniques to Disable Anyone in Seconds Using Minimal Force.* USA, 2009.

Planellas, Pau-Ramon. *Jintai Kyusho.* Barcelona, 1996.

Footnote References

1. http://www.iasp-pain.org//AM/Template.cfm?Section=Home

2. This is one of the problems of using Kyusho in a stress situation of an attack.

3. A balanced description of the placebo effect can be found in Ben Goldacre's book: Bad Science, Sept 2008.

4. Compare, for example, *Profil No 48* from 26.11.2007.

5. In our case, one has to speak of a "nocebo" effect that is often described as a negative placebo effect. This is where fears are built in the patient's mind, and he is made ill by external influences. Such persons actually then get ill or their appropriate symptoms can be observed and measured. An extreme example could be, for example, the death sentence imposed by the voodoo priest. Here it is imagined that the victim, in good faith, becomes ill with resignation and fear and then actually dies.

6. Michael Kelly's book, 2001, Page 13.

7. Throughout Michael Kelly's book, 2001.

8. Michael Kelly's book, 2001, Page 108.

9. According to an Austrian prosecutor, consent to such severe damage to health would not be legally possible and therefore disallowable. The suspect would have to reckon with criminal action.

10. Michael Kelly's book, 2001, Page 4.

11. Mark Link of Tufts New England Medical Center in Boston; see also New Scientist, August 30, 2003, pp. 38-39, under the title "Lethal Impact."

12. See also writings by Michael Kelly, 2001, p 102.

13. See Michael Kelly, 2001, p 21 et seq.

14. See Michael Kelly, 2001, p 91.

Weblinks

There are links that provide good anatomical illustrations and descriptions about Kyusho:
http://www.youtube.com/watch?v=SHtLlzw5zAE
http://www.youtube.com/watch?v=k0gjvTsftf0&feature=channel
http://www.youtube.com/watch?v=MinHtFAOOKA&feature=channel
http://www.youtube.com/watch?v=-_0PY2PtOJs&feature=channel
http://www.youtube.com/watch?v=BiiSAZkkxyA&feature=channel
http://www.youtube.com/watch?v=83p0MiOtnB0&feature=channel
http://www.youtube.com/watch?v=ZxpacPHE1-c&feature=channel
http://www.youtube.com/watch?v=tMQuU5pFbog&feature=channel
http://www.youtube.com/watch?v=9BUAXFZYXxl&feature=channel
http://www.youtube.com/watch?v=GBxsQqfIYFY&feature=channel
http://www.youtube.com/watch?v=Cvozl45O63I&feature=channel
http://www.youtube.com/watch?v=bsR3A3VFXBk&feature=channel
http://www.youtube.com/watch?v=5UAvIHnz_bM&feature=channel
http://www.youtube.com/watch?v=G3Efb0jvbjA&feature=channel
http://www.youtube.com/watch?v=tsWAG8igCc4&feature=channel
http://www.youtube.com/watch?v=Gekkq0Ofh3A&feature=channel
http://www.youtube.com/watch?v=HMd2Q7tfStw&p=065F44B8B598A9A1&playnext=1&index=4
http://www.youtube.com/watch?v=Trg0yZ65Qp8&feature=channel
http://www.youtube.com/watch?v=XN9PCc4166k&feature=channel
http://www.youtube.com/watch?v=PoOSklOGK3s&feature=channel
http://www.youtube.com/watch?v=SBzxL8oEdWQ&feature=channel

Picture Acknowledgements

Diagrams 1, 2, 4, 5, 7, 8, 9, 12, 14, 15, 17, 18, 19, 21, 22, 24, 25, 26, 27, 28, 29, 30, 31, 32, 33, 34, 35, 36, 37, 38 have been adapted for this book from http:www. wikipedia.de; therefore, the following statement is valid:

The faithful reproduction of a lithograph plate from Gray's Anatomy, a two-dimensional work of art, is not copyrightable in the U.S. as per Bridgeman Art Library v. Corel Corp.; the same is also true in many other countries, including Germany. Unless stated otherwise, it is from the 20th U.S. edition of Gray's Anatomy of the Human Body, originally published in 1918 and therefore lapsed into the public domain. Other copies of Gray's Anatomy can be found on Bartleby and Yahoo! These images are in the public domain because their copyright has expired. This applies worldwide.

Diagrams 3, 6, 10, 13, 16, 20, 23; with permission of Elsevier Limited, these have been adapted from the German language version of:
Drake, Vogl, Mitchel, Gray's Anatomie für Studenten (Gray's Anatomy for Students) (translated and published by Friedrich Paulsen), 1st Edition, 2007, © Elsevier GmbH, München, Urban & Fischer Verlag
Diagram 3 corresponds to Illustration 8.58, p 849, Head and neck
Diagram 6: Illustration 8.19, p 797, Head and neck
Diagram 10: Illustration 8.163, p 948, Head and neck
Diagram 13: Illustration 7.34, p 656, Upper Extremities
Diagram 16: Illustration 4.2, p 228, Abdomen
Diagram 20: Illustration 3.27, p 131, Thorax
Diagram 23: Illustration 4.110, p 319, Abdomen

Diagram 11: www.logopaediewiki.de/wiki/Larynx

Cover Photos: Alexandra Runge; © Hemera/Thinkstock
All other photos: Harald Marek
Head margin: © iStockphoto/Thinkstock
Cover Design: Sabine Groten

Legal notice

Please note that the usage of the exercises presented in this book will be at your own risk. Meyer&Meyer Sports GmbH and the authors will not be liable in any way (including for negligence) for any injury, loss, damage, costs or expenses suffered by using the exercises in this book.

For further legal information regarding the use of the exercises given in this book, please refer to the respective law of your country.

Christian Braun
Fitness for Fighters

Physical fitness is essential in order to be successful in martial arts. Martial arts practitioners must have flexible bodies and be capable of reacting quickly, they must have sufficient build and strength to carry out the lifts and throws, and they should have good stamina and coordination.

360 pages, full-color print, 1,484 photos
Paperback, 6 ½" x 9 ¼"
ISBN: 9781841262796
$19.95 US

Christian Braun
Free Fight
The Ultimate Guide to No-Holds-Barred Fighting

In the martial arts scene, Free Fight, or Mixed Martial Arts (No-Holds-Barred Fighting), is becoming more and more popular. Christian Braun shows you a realistic way to maintain and improve your chances in free fight. Techniques covering all disciplines and levels are included.

352 pages, full-color print, 1,258 photos
Paperback, 6 ½" x 9 ¼"
ISBN: 9781841262178
$ 19.95 US

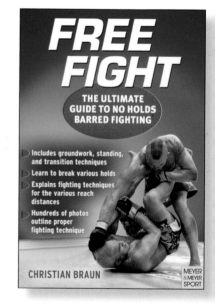

For more books visit

www.m-m-sports.com

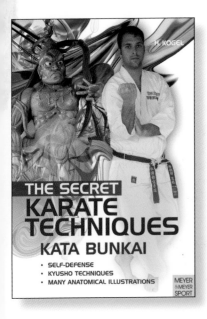

Helmut Kogel
The Secret Karate Techniques
Kata Bunkai

The varied facets of Karate first become obvious to the karate student after many years of intensive training and study of the roots of Okinawa's Martial Arts. This book guides you through the theoretical and historical background and the practice of the so-called secret techniques.

248 pages, full-color print, 486 photos, 3 illus.
Paperback, 6 ½" x 9 ¼"
ISBN: 9781841262895
E-Book: 9781841267562
$19.95US

Arnaud van der Veere
Muay Thai

The book shows the basics of the challenging sport Muay Thai. Learn the techniques and understand how to apply them. Numerous exercises guarantee a varied and interesting training. Besides the total workout of the body, the sport improves personal awareness, stamina and physical control.

192 pages, full-color print, 700 photos
Paperback, 6 ½" x 9 ¼"
ISBN: 9781841263281
E-Book: 9781841264165
$ 18.95 US

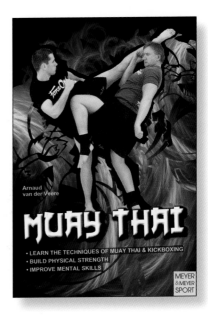

All books available as E-books.

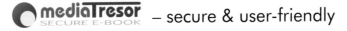 – secure & user-friendly

MEYER & MEYER SPORT